The Great MOUNTAIN *to* MOUNTAIN *Safari*

Kilimanjaro – Table Mountain – Kilimanjaro

ALSO BY CINDY VINE

Stop the world, I need to pee!

The Case of Billy B

Not Telling

WRITTEN AS CINDY VAN DEN HEUVEL

Fear, Phobias and Frozen Feet

www.cindyvine.com

Cover design by Cris Advincula

The Great
MOUNTAIN
to
MOUNTAIN
Safari

Cindy Vine
Photographs by Cindy Vine and
Siobhan Kedian

Disclaimer

All descriptions, characters, and details are purely fictitious, and a product of my imagination.

Copyright © Cindy Vine 2010

The moral right of the author has been asserted.

ISBN is 1453853294
EAN-13 is 9781453853290

Printed in USA by Createspace

This book is dedicated to my children, Kerri, Tony and Siobhan who have accompanied me on many adventures and always held my hand whenever I got scared.

Acknowledgements

Thanks to my editor, Robert Stark, who checks my grammar and spelling, and always manages to lift me up when I am down.

Thanks to my friends who supported me, gave me travel tips, armed me with weapons and checked in with me all the way.

Thanks to all the wonderful people we met along the way, for helping to make this safari so awesome. Your helpfulness and friendliness was much appreciated, and cancelled out any tiredness I might have been feeling.

Thanks to the good Lord above for keeping us safe.

And the largest thanks of all goes to my daughter Siobhan, who entertained me, waited on me by passing me snacks and drinks, kept me focused, and proved to be the best travel partner ever. Many of the photos used in this book were taken by Siobhan along the way. She supported me with my idea to turn our safari into a guide book of sorts, and went out of her way to try and take the best photos imaginable. Siobhan also had the idea to keep a video diary of our trip, which can be seen on YouTube. Siobhan, you are the bomb!

Africa

——— UP TRIP

——— DOWN TRIP

Contents

Introduction

An old fuel-guzzling car with a reconditioned engine, an open African road, a passport, a moody teenager and a weak bladder – what more do you need to undertake a road trip of a lifetime?

Somewhere in my genetic make-up, must be an explorer gene. The desire to visit faraway places, discover new holiday destinations and experience different cultures seems to be an integral part of my psyche. The urge to travel is too strong to resist. Unfortunately for my children, over the years I've forced them to accompany me on my many adventures. Now, with just one child left in the nest, one has to be more creative with family holidays, seeing that it's just Siobhan and me left to carry on with our family tradition of exciting and very different holidays. We've never done the normal family holiday thing, of jetting off to a luxury resort, as money has always been a little tight. Single mother, three children, no child support – you get the picture. With plane tickets very expensive for the duration of the 2010 Football World Cup held in South Africa, it was time to get creative. So, I came up with the idea of driving down to Cape Town from Moshi in Tanzania.

There wasn't enough time to do proper research as the power supply in Moshi was going through one of its erratic phases, and internet connectivity was intermittent at best. The usual end of school year jobs made life hectic and time was at a premium. So, it was with a little trepidation that I climbed into my car on the Saturday at noon to head off south, not knowing exactly where I was headed or where we would be staying, just that in a week or so we would hopefully arrive in Cape Town. In fact, other than a few comments on blogs, there wasn't too much information about a trip like this, and guide books didn't give me the information that I needed. Then again, most guide books are written by men who don't think of mentioning the important things, like where one can find a decent toilet en route.

I did manage to get my car serviced with new oil and fuel filters and an oil change. Not knowing that much about cars, I thought that should suffice. For the record, my car is a 1994 Pajero with a reconditioned Toyota 2 litre petrol engine in it. So half of the car is geared towards diesel and the other half for petrol. A bit confusing if you're not a mechanic. All I know is that when I drive uphill the car struggles as the engine is not really strong enough for the weight of the car. Other than that, I thought the trip shouldn't be a problem as the car was mostly reliable. The choke didn't work, but as Tanzania is quite a hot country, and that hadn't proved to be something major in the past. I reckoned it would be okay. I'd last changed a car tyre in about 1996, but thought if a tyre did blow and I stood next to the car and looked helpless enough, someone would help if the need arose. I did have the foresight to check that I had a jack and I bought a wheel spanner when I noticed that mine was missing. Equipped with an old rusted jerry can, both a foam- and a dry-powder fire extinguisher, and two road triangles, I felt well-equipped for a road trip of this magnitude. The night before we quickly packed our bags and cooked a lamb roast which we could put on bread rolls I'd planned to buy along the way.

I forgot to mention that two days before we left, one of the parents of a child in my class approached me with a black supermarket bag. "I've been worrying about your trip down, a woman and child travelling alone is not good. So, I've brought you some weapons." Inside the bag was a tazer that looked like a mobile phone and a small box holding a pepper-spray gun. "You'll be safe with these," the father said lifting his weapons out of the bag. "When someone approaches and asks for your mobile phone, hand him this but point it at his balls and press this button." A huge crackling spark came out of the mobile phone look-alike. "Guaranteed to knock the assailant flying and stop him from producing any more children." I nodded my head, too scared to touch a mobile phone that could send out such a dangerous spark. He lifted up the small box and opened it. Inside was a very realistic looking gun. "There's only two shots in this gun, so you have to make them count. The bonus is that you'll turn your assailant orange, so that he's easy to pick out in a police line-up." With big eyes I nodded my thanks and carefully took the black bag with the weapons inside. Now that I was armed to the teeth with weapons of ass destruction, I knew that I was definitely prepared for the trip.

It was only after several hundred kilometres of driving, that I got the idea to write a book about the trip. When you have a teenager singing next to you, you tend to zone out and think of other things. I thought about the books I'd written and published, further ideas for other books, and then it suddenly struck me. If I hadn't found much resource material about a trip like this, then other people contemplating this trip would also be struggling to find information. Why not, keep a diary, record everything, take photos and have a handy guide for others thinking about undertaking a trip such as this? The more I thought about it, the more I liked the idea, and somewhere between Moshi and Morogoro, 'The Great Mountain-to-Mountain Safari' was born.

I wanted this guide to be unlike any other. Inside, besides my route, places to stay at or visit along the way, I've also included boxes with random factoids and cool recipes to try from each country I visited. Oh, and most importantly - where to find a decent toilet on the road!

At the time of our trip these were the exchange rates and I've used them in this guide to convert local currency to US$.

1 US$ = R7.69 (South Africa) 1 US$ = 5130 Zambian Kwacha
1 US$ = 7.06 Pula (Botswana) 1 US$ = 1505 Shillings (Tanzania)
1 US$ = 149.80 Malawian Kwacha

Happy travelling!
Safari Njema!
Cindy Vine

TANZANIA

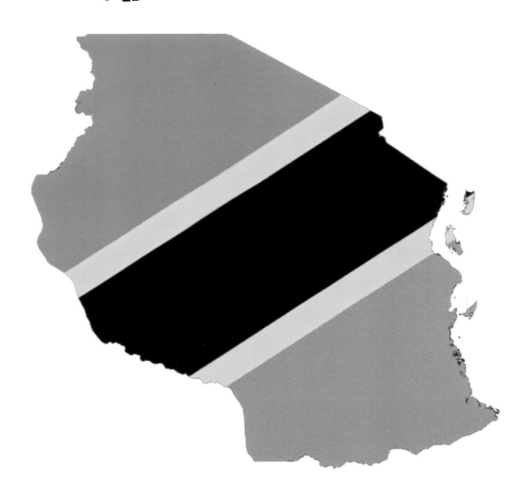

Kilimanjaro to Table Mountain

Day One: Moshi to Morogoro

Savour every moment, good and bad, as you never know when you may experience it again.

For a couple of weeks we'd been cooking all the meat in the freezer, so as not to leave anything frozen while we were away which might defrost during a power cut. There is nothing worse than returning home after a lovely holiday, and being greeted by the stench of rotting meat. The rotting meat smell has the ability to permeate every pore and destroys all memories of sun-tanning on a beach in an exotic location. The plan was to leave the leg of lamb for the night before the trip. I'd cook it, carve it up and use it to make sandwiches along the way. The leg of lamb always seemed to be something in the not-too distant future; a marker to the start of our trip. Before I realised it, the leg of lamb was the only item in the freezer and it was time to cook it. The trip had crept up on us, tip-toeing through the busy end-of-school year jobs that take over your life and your thoughts. As I prepared the lamb roast and banged it into the oven, it struck me that I had not yet gotten around to doing any research for the trip. In fact, I hadn't even considered yet, what we were going to be taking with us and which suitcases we were going to use! Talk about being disorganised, that's probably the understatement of the year.

With the lamb roast sending delicious cooking smells around the house, I quickly hopped onto the internet to do a little research. Unfortunately, nothing much came up. The occasional blog but none of the details I really needed, like distances between towns so that I could get an idea of when I'd be able to fill up my very thirsty car. This did make me a little nervous as I had visions of us being stranded in the middle of nowhere without a petrol station in sight. I quickly looked through online maps and worked out the route we'd take, making notes of towns we could stop at for the night. Not being too flush with cash, the accommodations would have to be within our very limited budget.

The next morning, Saturday, we loaded our small suitcases we'd hastily packed first thing that morning into the car. The lock on the boot door decided to pack in just then, preventing us from opening it. Left with a decision of lifting all suitcases over the back seat into the boot and having to repeat the performance each stop, or just putting them on the back seat and forgetting about the boot; we chose the latter. I didn't want any added grief on such a long trip. I stashed the empty jerry can behind my seat, and the fire extinguishers and road triangles behind Siobhan's seat. The cooler box was filled with the sliced roast lamb wrapped in tinfoil, some juices and apples, and we were ready to hit the road. Being me, of course, nothing was pre-booked. My thought was, we'd find a place to stay when we arrived at each day's destination. Unfortunately, school required us to work the morning as part of their in-service programme, so even though my car was packed and I was psyched up to leave, I couldn't. It did make it all a little frustrating.

Mount Kilimanjaro. The mountain is made up of three volcanic cones. It is the tallest freestanding mountain rise in the world, and the highest mountain in Africa. Uhuru Peak is the highest summit of Mount Kilimanjaro at 5895km. Although many people think that part of Mount Kilimanjaro is in Kenya, in actual fact it is situated entirely within the borders of Tanzania. Kibo, the highest volcanic cone, is classed as a dormant active volcano and climbers can smell sulphur emanating from the inner ash pit. What makes Kilimanjaro so interesting to climb, is that it contains virtually every ecosystem on earth – glacier, snowfields, deserts, alpine moorland, savannah, and tropical jungle, all of which found on the mountain. Of the 30 000 odd people who start the climb annually, only 60% reach the summit. 8-9 Climbers die each year, succumbing to acute mountain sickness from failing to acclimatise to the high altitude.

Finally, at 11h45 we were able to leave. A quick look at Mount Kilimanjaro with its ice caps towering behind us and we were ready to start our adventure. My usual fuel station had a queue of cars, so I decided to start the drive and fill up somewhere along the way. Just stopping off first at the bakery in Moshi town to pick up some freshly baked bread rolls, we were soon on our way - feeling both excited and a little apprehensive. Once when we'd lived in Botswana, I'd driven 3000km in a long weekend visiting Zimbabwe. I'd also taken three days to drive from Umtata in the Transkei, to Swakopmund in Nambia. But those trips paled into insignificance when I contemplated the trip ahead. With nobody to share the driving load with me, no convoy of cars as support vehicles behind me, it did appear to be a daunting task. Frankly, I wasn't sure I'd be able to do it. Of course, I didn't share those fears with my daughter, who was already trying to recline her seat next to me and make herself comfortable. I had to come across as this confident adult who knew exactly what she was doing.

It seemed that every trucking company in Tanzania had heard that we were hitting the road, as they sent out every slow-moving truck in their stable to lead our way. Overtaking is often a challenge in Tanzania, not just because of potholes and animals, but also because of the frequent changes in speed limits and traffic police looking more like they belonged to the Royal Navy, waiting in unmarked cars to nab you when you drove over the speed limit. Then of course, there are the speeding buses heading straight towards you, who never seem to get caught for speeding, although you do come across the occasional wrecks of those that got a wobble and overturned.

We stopped off at Same, just over 100km from Moshi, and filled up the car with petrol. Amazingly, the traffic police were having a Saturday off and we never encountered a single road block the whole of the first day, which is very strange for Tanzania. Maybe they were all sitting in a pub watching a World Cup Football game on television. The road from Momba to Segera was very bad, with us playing an 'avoid the pothole' game. You have to weave across the road to try and escape from disappearing inside big craters in the road. Okay, maybe that's a slight exaggeration, but just know the potholes on that stretch are pretty bad.

From Segera, the road improved and we were able to play a game of Travel Scrabble. Somehow or other, I had picked up a set of French Travel Scrabble, so the scoring on the letters was different to the English one, but it still worked. I managed to drop the tiny letter tiles on the floor on only three occasions, which had Siobhan scrabbling to try and find them and cursing under her breath, giving me evil looks. Luckily, over the years I've become immune to 'the look.' Siobhan, to her credit, did manage to make me the most delicious roast lamb bread rolls along the way.

About 100km from Morogoro, Siobhan started reading our Tanzanian Guide Book to try and find a suitable place to stay. Unfortunately, it was dark when we reached Morogoro, and we were unable to find any of the hotels she'd picked. Later on in the trip, we found out that she was reading the maps incorrectly, so we were always heading in the opposite direction to what was given on the map.

Now my bladder is a little weird. It seems to sense when a potential toilet is near. We had travelled over 500km, during that time I had no desire to go to the bathroom, but the minute we stopped outside our first potential motel I had to go so badly I could hardly walk. I think it's a gravity thing. The minute you get down from the car and stand next to it, urine collected inside your bladder drops to the valve, putting pressure on it to open and let it out. So walking with my knees clamped together, I finally made it to the motel reception. I could feel sweat beginning to form on my brow from the exertion of keeping my legs clamped tight. Unfortunately, they were fully booked, but they did let me use their toilet.

With my eyeballs no longer floating, I was able to focus more on finding us a suitable place to stay. We'd given up on Siobhan's suggestions, as we couldn't even find the road they were on in the dark. I noticed a sign saying 'Rhino Motel,' and we decided to see if they had any rooms available. Luckily they had rooms and the room rate was much cheaper than I had anticipated. The room was basic with a double bed, and we thought Siobhan and I could share no problem. However, the receptionist with her very limited English had other ideas. She forbade us to share a room. We each had to have separate rooms. Siobhan was too scared to sleep alone, the reception area and motel was a little seedy, but the receptionist was adamant. We had to take two separate rooms, on opposite sides of the motel. As I was tired and the rooms were so cheap, I paid for two even though we used only one. Bizarre, but what can I say? These things happen. As The Rhino Motel had no restaurant, we ate some more bread rolls filled with roast lamb from our stash. I was starting to get a little sick of roast lamb, but it was on our menu for breakfast as well. One good thing about the Rhino Motel; it is on the highway, and has very secure parking with a big steel gate and 24 hour guard. The bed was comfortable; we managed a good night's sleep, although the bathroom was not the nicest we were to find on our trip.

RECIPES FROM AFRICA – Tanzania

Beef Stew

This easy to make delicious stew will have your mouth watering as the sensational cooking smells seep up your nostrils. It serves 4-6, but is so tasty you might want to double up as everybody will want seconds!

Ingredients

2 tablespoons cooking oil

500g beef cut into cubes

1 large onion cut into rings

6 tomatoes finely chopped

1 cup coconut milk

1 tablespoon finely chopped coriander leaves

1 chilli finely chopped

Salt and pepper to taste

Method: Heat the oil in a pot with a lid. Brown the beef and the onion rings. Throw in the rest of the ingredients and leave to simmer for about 45 minutes on a low heat until the meat is cooked and falling apart. Serve with a hefty spoonful of Mataha.

Mataha

This is a great variation on the old mashed potato recipe. It serves 4-6 and is great with stews and casseroles.

Ingredients

2 cups fresh or frozen peas

2 cups corn from the cob

5 potatoes

2 tablespoons cooking oil

Salt and pepper to taste

Method: Boil vegetables separately until cooked. Mash the potatoes. Put the cooking oil into a frying pan, and add the peas, corn and mashed potato. Heat through and mix until all the ingredients are mashed together. Serve with your meat dish.

**Rhino Motel
Morogoro
Tanzania**

From the outside it appeared okay as it had secure parking and a guard.
Inside was very basic. The receptionist spoke limited English.
The room was nothing to get excited about. The en suite was below standard and the television locked in a cage probably describes the usual clientele. Breakfast was not included. In fact there was no restaurant on the premises so meals were not available.
However, the bed was comfortable and at only $8 a night, this was an affordable option.

Stats for the day					
Odometer Start	**Odometer Finish**	**Day's Kilometres**	**Depart Time**	**Arrive Time**	**Hours travel**
176 301	176 867	566	11h45	18h45	7 hours
Fuel	**Cost local currency**	**Cost US$**	**Accommodation**	**Cost local currency**	**Cost US$**
78.70 litres	133000 TSH	$88.37	Rhino Motel, Morogoro	12000 TSH	$7.97

Day Two: Morogoro to Mbeya

After a comfortable night's sleep where Siobhan stole all the blankets only about three times - and left me clinging to the edge of the bed trying not to fall off while she spread herself out like a starfish - we were ready to roll. We decided to give the shower a miss because it was only cold water. Sniffing, the lamb, it seemed to have survived the night in the cooler box, and we were able to use the last of the bread rolls to make roast lamb rolls for breakfast to eat in the car.

We left at 7am on the dot, excited as we felt our big trip was really starting now. The previous day had just been a warm-up as we had driven that road a few times before. This road, however, was completely new to us, and we felt a bit like modern-day explorers heading into the unknown. As you can tell, it doesn't take much to get us excited.

Sometimes in life it is hard to be an adult. You have to make decisions all the time. Your children seem to think you know all the answers and making these decisions is easy. From time to time I do make wrong decisions. Deciding not to fill up the fuel tank in Morogoro was one of my wrong decisions.

Uluguru Mountains

The **Uluguru Mountains** behind Morogoro rise to over 2600m. They are the home of the Luguru People for the past 300 years, who were regularly raided for slaves by a man called Kisabengo, who built a fortified village for supplying the slave traders at what is now known as Morogoro. The Uluguru Mountains have become renowned for their unique biodiversity and the fact that many of the plant and animal species found in the sub-montane forests there are found nowhere else in the world.

The cool thing about driving from Morogoro to Mbeya, is that the highway goes through the Mikumi National Park. You have 50km of amazing game viewing. We took our time driving through the park, eyes on high alert to see who spotted game first. Siobhan won hands down as I did have to watch the road as well. I did, however, spot a dead hyena on the side of the road, obviously a road kill. The trucks and buses blaze through the park at a furious pace, having no interest in viewing the game. I imagine that quite a lot of game end up like that hyena. We saw a herd of elephant heading through the thick bush on the side of the road, and by the time I'd pulled the car to the side of the road so Siobhan could take photos, all we could see were their bottoms moving through the vegetation. Luckily, we soon saw herds of buffalo, different buck, zebra and a few groups of giraffe, so Siobhan's sulking at my failure to stop quickly enough for the elephant photo soon evaporated. Although, looking through our photos we did seem to develop a penchant for bottoms!

11

About 20km from the park exit, I suddenly became aware of the fact that my fuel gauge was on empty. Visions of being stuck in the park, trampled by elephants and eaten by lions came into my mind. Quite stupidly, I might add, because there was quite a bit of traffic going through the park. Someone would have helped us, wouldn't they? But with an over-active imagination, worse-case scenarios do tend to spring to mind. I decided not to tell Siobhan that she might have many hours of snapping animals if we ran out of fuel, and instead stopped trying to spot game and rather channelled all my energy and thoughts into willing my car to drive on the smell of an oil rag. As the fuel light came on, a road sign appeared before us saying, '2km to Mikumi.'

After my initial euphoria that there was a town that we would just make it to before the fuel ran out, reality hit. There might not necessary be a fuel station in the town. We had passed other towns earlier without fuel stations. Anxiety returned for the next 2km while I debated whether to keep both hands on the steering wheel or chew my nails nervously. My fears were allayed when a fuel station loomed before us and I'm sure I even heard my car sigh with relief.

The road from Morogoro through Mikumi had been really good and we never spotted a single road block. The landscape changed quite dramatically; baobabs replaced the bushveld, and the terrain became more mountainous. Baboons were the next wildlife to appear. Troops of them on the road, some sitting in trees. Siobhan had great fun throwing the apples I'd bought for the trip out of the window. The very same apples which are so expensive to buy in Tanzania. She also threw out the avocado pear from the tree in my garden which was very green when I'd packed it in the cooler box two nights before and had since ripened to a very soft ready-to-burst avo. The baboons loved the treats, and one in particular galloped next to the car catching all the apples as Siobhan threw them out of the window. It was quite funny, as at one stage that particular baboon had an apple in each hand, two in its mouth and was still loping next to the car ready to grab a fifth.

The road works several kilometres before Iringa slowed us down considerably, as on many occasions you have to sit and wait for about twenty minutes until all oncoming traffic has passed before you are allowed to go. Feeling sorry for one of the traffic controllers who looked tired and had sweat dripping down his neck, we gave him the last of our roast lamb, bread rolls and a juice.

I'd promised Siobhan a good lunch in Iringa. Iringa wasn't that easy to find as some of the road signs had been removed with all the road works. We actually drove past the turn-off and found ourselves in the Iringa Industrial Area which is at the bottom of a hill. An attendant at a fuel station quickly pointed us in the right direction, and we took the turn-off to Iringa Town which is perched on the top of a very steep hill. My car struggled a bit up the hill and this was further aggravated by the road works which meant that you could never go fast enough to get some momentum going. Once we reached Iringa at exactly twelve noon, we soon discovered a new problem. It was a Sunday and everything seemed to be shut on a Sunday. Siobhan's promised lunch might not be an eventuality - gone along with the promise of a decent toilet which we'd hoped to find at a restaurant. Kindly giving away the roast lamb remnants might not have been a good idea after all. However, someone directed us to the main street and a little restaurant called Hasty Tasty, so it seemed we would be able to get something to eat.

Hasty Tasty lived up to its name; the menu looked great with a good selection of meals and after placing our order, I asked if they had a bathroom. I was directed down a suspect alley to the back of the building, where there were plenty of ramshackle outbuildings in different stages of disrepair. As luck would have it, the outhouse with the dodgy wooden door and toilet sign was occupied, and I hopped around a little with my knees clamped shut debating on whether or not to quickly go behind another corrugated iron shack. As I was going to drop my pants and expose my large white bottom for the world to see, the toilet door which had only one remaining hinge was pushed open, and a large man made his way out, the fumes of something that had crawled up his bottom and died following him. He had flushed I suppose, although the squatter toilet boasted skid marks like none other seen before. I could feel myself beginning to gag at the stench and I hadn't even entered the stall yet. Holding my nose after taking a deep breath, I managed to slide the catch shut and drop my pants with one hand, do my deed, pull up my pants and leave – all without taking a breath. To say that toilet was disgusting was the understatement of the year. By the time I stumbled through the litter and shrubs of the alley to make my way back to Siobhan who was waiting patiently for her turn to use the bathroom, our food had arrived. I advised her to rather be brave and hold her bladder than use that bathroom. But other than the sub-standard toilet, Hasty Tasty was good value for money. The food was very tasty.

Across from Hasty Tasty was an Internet Cafe and Information Point. We decided to head over and see if they had a better toilet as Siobhan's eyeballs were starting to float. The outside of the shop didn't prepare us for what was inside. A coffee shop where you could order cakes and cappuccinos as well as food from Hasty Tasty; a great book shop; garden and fantastic modern bathrooms with clean flush toilets! I ordered a cappuccino while Siobhan used the bathroom and I browsed the books eventually selecting a Zambian Travel Guide. I thought it might be a good idea as I didn't even know the name of the first town we'd be heading to on the Zambian side! I did say there'd been no time for proper research! From the Information Desk, we got directions to a place where we'd be able to buy the special reflector stickers needed in Zambia, and these we picked up on the way out of Iringa along with several new-release DVDS illegally imported from China and a large blue plastic funnel. If I filled the jerry can with petrol it wouldn't be much use without a funnel to pour it into the car with, hence the purchase.

We left Iringa at 2.30pm and continued with our drive to Mbeya. Surprisingly enough, we never saw a police road block the entire day, which is highly unusual for Tanzania.

Somewhere between Iringa and Mbeya, Siobhan discovered her fascination with her own body parts, and this fascination was to continue for the rest of our trip, as she pulled faces and took photos of herself. I guess that it was good that she found a way to keep herself from getting bored, as there is nothing worse than travelling with a bored and disgruntled teenager.

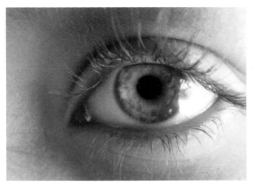 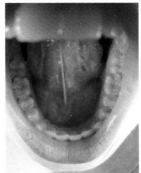

It was 6.45pm when we pulled into Mbeya it was already dark. Siobhan was trying to read the instructions on how to get to a hotel she'd selected from the guide book. After driving up and down the main road several times, we came to the conclusion that she actually had no idea where we were. In desperation, we turned down a random road that looked important as there were quite a few cars on it, and accidentally found the first hotel we'd been trying to find and had given up on.

The Rift Valley Hotel looked quite imposing in the dark. It had a nice secure car park with a high fence, 24 hour guard and a lockable gate. Inside, the hotel had seen better days, being a little seedy and rundown. However, the guy at the reception was very friendly and helpful and let us use the bathroom next to their bar before checking in. I don't know what it is about hotel receptions, but the minute I stand in one to check in, I have an overwhelming urge to pee.

The room was nice enough, although they forgot to give us towels and I had to go down to ask for toilet paper. It seemed as if we were the only guests at the hotel. We went downstairs to order some dinner. Although the waiting time was unbearably long, it was worth it in the end as the food was obviously freshly cooked. We had the best homemade tomato soup I have ever eaten for starters, and deliciously tender chunks of beef curry and rice for mains. Definitely worth the long wait. Back in our room, Siobhan was excited to find that they had cable television. As I said before, it doesn't take much to get us excited!

In 2005 a new species of monkey was discovered in the mountains close to Mbeya. The medium-sized primate has been named the **highland mangabey** and its thick brown fur shows that it has specially adapted to living in a high mountain habitat where temperatures can drop to below freezing. The highland mangabey is characterised by an off-white tail and belly, an upright crest on its head and a strange low honk-bark which is unlike the call made by any other primate.

Rift Valley Hotel
Mbeya Tanzania

This hotel must have been very grand when it was new. Now it is a little run down. The staff are very friendly and speak excellent English. There's no complimentary tea and coffee in the room and they forgot to supply us with a towel. A continental breakfast is included. There's a good restaurant, but be prepared to wait for your food. $20 a night.

Stats for the day					
Odometer Start	**Odometer Finish**	**Day's Kilometres**	**Depart Time**	**Arrive Time**	**Hours travel**
176 867	177 548	681	07h00	18h45	11h45
Fuel	**Cost local currency**	**Cost US$**	**Accommodation**	**Cost local currency**	**Cost US$**
111.73 litres	183500 TSH	$121.93	Rift Valley Hotel, Mbeya	30000TSH	$19.93

ZAMBIA

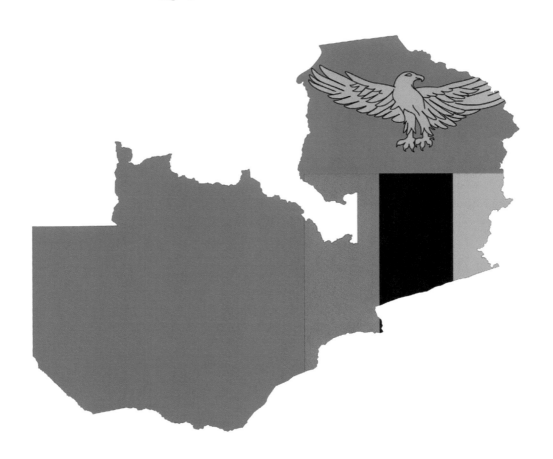

If I didn't admit to being nervous about entering Zambia, I'd be lying. I'd heard so many negative reports about corrupt policemen manning Zambian road blocks. So it was probably with some relief that we decided to give up waiting for our eggs to arrive. Those eggs wouldn't have sat well with my nervous stomach anyway. For some strange reason Siobhan was convinced that we were getting a Full English Breakfast at the Rift Valley Hotel. I had just heard them say breakfast included, not what type of breakfast, but that with Siobhan means eggs, bacon and toast. Imagine her disappointment when they put a flask of hot milky ginger tea on the table and brought us some mango and bananas. Of all the fruits on Planet Earth, those are her least favourite. She handed me her mango and nibbled on her banana with long teeth and a sick smile. After a while, they brought us each a thick slice of homemade bread, and carefully scraped some butter and a dollop of jam onto a saucer for us. Siobhan sat waiting for her egg while I tucked into my lovely fresh slice of bread. It was more a doorstop than a slice! I was dying for a coffee, really needed some caffeine to kick-start my day, but that had obviously gone the way of the egg. After what seemed like a good half hour had passed, Siobhan finally conceded that the egg was not going to magically appear, and ate her bread. We hit the road at 8.30am, ready for the day's adventures.

After no sign of any police road blocks the previous day, we managed to go through four different road blocks between Mbeya and the Zambian border. Luckily, all they wanted to know was where we came from and where we were going to. When they heard we were headed to Cape Town, they became very friendly, joked about the Football World Cup, and wished us a very safe journey.

We finally arrived at the border at 10am, completely unprepared for the chaos that greeted us. As the car ground to a halt we were mobbed by men of all ages, shapes and sizes, some waving fistfuls of kwacha, US dollars, others with official looking papers. It was madness and quite frightening. I shooed them away as one does flies and went into the customs and immigration building. Of course, you can never be sure of which queue to wait in as the people who work there are not always the most helpful. A little man with an official-looking light-blue shirt, dark blue tie and a name badge attached himself onto us and took charge. He said he worked for Customs. As he looked the part I believed him, and we quickly sailed through the different queues. When we arrived back at our car, another official-looking man was waiting next to it, the partner of the man in the blue shirt and tie. "I'll be your agent in Zambia," he said with authority. I looked at him in disbelief. I had distinctly repeated over and over again as we were being mobbed when we first arrived, that we did not want an agent.

"Sorry, we do not need an agent, please leave us alone,' I repeated firmly about three times while the agent made as if to climb into our car.

The man in the blue shirt and tie smiled. "It's okay he's my partner. I do the Tanzanian side and he does the Zambian side."

I could feel the blood begin to boil in my ears and I'm sure smoke was starting to puff out my nostrils. We'd been duped! The helpful little guy who worked for Customs was actually an agent in disguise! "I said I don't want an agent. You said you were with Customs," I snarled at the smiling blue shirt man.

"No, not Customs," laughed the little man, "I'm an agent. I work with customs to help get you through. Now about my fee..."

"You are a lying little shit who tried to deceive me," I said through clenched teeth, "I said repeatedly I don't want an agent, you pretended to work for Customs. I haven't got any Tanzanian Shillings left so I wouldn't have hired you anyway. Get away from my car, I don't want an agent!"

As I slammed the door and drove off narrowly missing the agent's foot, I heard him shout, "If you don't have shillings it's okay, I take US Dollars!"

If I thought the Tanzanian side was bad with agents swarming like flies, the Zambian side was even worse. And, they don't take 'no' for an answer. They thrust themselves on you, invading your space, and I could see from Siobhan's face that she was terrified. Eventually, we managed to swat most of them out of the way although a few sticky ones still followed us. The immigration part was easy, just a stamp in our passports. The car part was a bit more complicated. We first had to show all the car's papers, then wait for it to be cleared by the Zambian CID. Then we had to queue

21

to pay the carbon tax which, when we finally got to the front of the queue, one can only pay in kwacha. Determined not to be stung by the agents' exchange rates as they waved bundles of kwacha at us, we walked up the hill to the Bureau d'Change and changed our dollars for kwacha over there. The carbon tax cost us 150 000 kwacha which is roughly US$30. We thought we were finished with the Zambian Border and high-fived each other as we walked to the car. How sadly mistaken we were. As we drove to the gate, past the rows and rows of dusty impounded cars, the guard asked for our Zambian Road Toll paper. I showed him the receipt for the carbon tax and he shook his head solemnly and pointed us back to the direction we'd just come from. I reversed the car, cursing all the while, drove back and parked expecting to be swarmed by agents again. This time they left us alone, still sulking that we hadn't taken advantage of their highly-inflated exchange rates. We eventually got directions to an old shipping container hidden somewhere behind the immigration buildings where we could buy the road tax. "Thirty US Dollars," the attendant said holding out his hand.

"How much in kwacha," I asked reaching into my wallet for kwacha.

"Sorry, no kwacha, we only take dollars," the man said waving me away and helping the person behind me. I couldn't believe this! So we trudged back up the hill to where we'd parked the car, retrieved some dollars from the hiding place in the car, and walked all the way back down to pay the Zambian Road Toll. Finally we were able to leave. The whole border crossing had taken us two and a half hours! To add insult to injury, nobody was manning the border gate when we drove through, so we didn't need to show our Zambian Road Toll!

We were in Zambia and it didn't feel any different to being in Tanzania. A man in a Bafana Bafana shirt blowing a vuvuzela was the first sign that we were heading closer to South Africa and the Football World Cup. The long straight road stretched ahead, at first there weren't too many of the fabled Zambian potholes and we made good time. The road was surprisingly quiet, which was strange after all the trucks we'd passed waiting at the border. Siobhan opened the Zambian travel Guide we'd bought the day before in Iringa, and we found the name of the first town where we'd be able to stop for fuel and hopefully some lunch – Isoka.

Isoka was a bit of a disappointment. One blink and you drove past it. We had to turn back to find the turn-off and drive down a dirt road to find the one and only fuel station, a Total Service Station. Although there were fuel pumps, the fuel attendant said that the fuel wasn't very good and he had better fuel locked up in barrels inside the back room. He filled a 30 litre container full of supposedly high-grade petrol for us, and poured it into our tank. I closed my eyes and prayed that the fuel was really high grade as the whole episode seemed a little suspect. Lord knows which fuel tanker that fuel had come from, but the car seemed to like it.

It was as we were leaving Isoka that Siobhan decided we had to give the car a name. After rejecting all my suggestions, she decided it had to have a feminine name, and Missy the Mitsubishi she became and still is.

With few villages, no traffic and hardly any people walking on the road, it was destined to be a long day with not much to break the tedium of the road. We entertained ourselves by making up silly rhyming songs but after an hour or so even that got stale. The potholes suddenly littered the

road like huge craters caused by aliens crashing their flying saucers. At some points, it was like driving through a warzone, and at others the road appeared to be newly tarred. One had to remain alert at all times as you never knew when the road would suddenly deteriorate into a minefield of potholes that you had to weave your way around. We had just decided that lunch was not going to be an option, when we drove into a tiny village with a take-away. We ordered fried chicken which had only just had the feathers removed, and was cooked in such a way that you couldn't tell what part was meat and what was bone, and watched some football on their large television screen. Definitely didn't expect to find satellite TV in a village in the wop-wops!

About an hour later, in the middle of nowhere, Siobhan decided that she had to pee. Waiting until the next town was not an option; it was an emergency. As I was sitting down, gravity didn't come into play with me and I was still okay. "Try and hold it in, " I suggested kindly with a smile. Siobhan just glared and her eyes welled with tears. "Well, what would you like me to do about it?" I asked, with a little more irritation than I should have.

"Stop the car now. I'll just go in the grass." And she did. Luckily, no vehicles or people appeared on the horizon.

So, if you travel this way make a note, there are no toilets between the border and Mpika.

When travelling through Isoka, you should detour to see the **Shiwa Ng'andu Manor House** which is named after the nearby lake which in Bemba means 'lake of the royal crocodile.' It was built in 1920 by Sir Stewart Gore-Browne who always wanted to live in a large house like the one owned by his aunt in Britain. Of course, it was far more expensive to build such a mansion in Britain. The building work on the manor house was only completed in the late fifties, so it was a lifetime project for Sir Stewart. The estate became like a Utopian self-contained town, with its own schools, hospitals, playing fields, shops, and even a post office. Sir Steart got involved in Zambian politics and when he died in 1967, he became the only white man in Zambia's history to be given a state funeral. In 1991 Sir Stewart's daughter and son-in-law who were running the estate after his death, were tragically murdered in Lusaka. The estate is still run by descendants of Gore-Browne and is now a bed and breakfast as well as a farming/safari business.

Somewhere along the way Siobhan read that Zambia was an hour behind Tanzania, so we duly moved Missy's clock back and reset our cellphones. We still seemed to be getting our Tanzanian signal.

We pulled into Mpika when it was still light at 5.30pm, and spotted the Mazinga Hotel on the left just before the main part of town. It had a high wall around the property, a metal gate with a security guard in attendance, and it looked all good. The rooms were in flamingo pink and baby blue blocks, and although basic were pretty clean and very comfortable. We ordered dinner to be sent to our rooms from the restaurant next to the reception, and waited two hours for it finally to arrive. Siobhan had beef stew and rice and I had beef stew with nshima, the delicious maize meal staple of Zambia. Dinner was really good, huge portions and very filling, which I guess it would have to be after a two-hour wait!

RECIPES FROM AFRICA - Zambia

Futari

This great dish goes well with a barbecue and will help build your reputation as the BBQ specialist in your area. It serves 8, so invite all your friends!

Ingredients

6 cups water
2kg peeled and thinly sliced sweet potatoes
Salt to taste
Peanut Sauce
4 cups ground peanuts
1 cup hot water

Method

Boil the slices of sweet potato in the water. Drain the cooked sweet potato slices and arrange the slices in a greased baking dish. Season with salt. Make your peanut sauce by mixing the ground peanuts together with the cup of boiling water in a small bowl. Pour the sauce on the sweet potatoes. Bake at 180 degrees Celsius or 350 degrees Fahrenheit for 15 minutes.

Imphwa

Especially for the vegetarians out there, see – I didn't forget you! This dish is great with rice or maize meal porridge. It serves 8.

Ingredients

2 cups water
3 onions coarsely chopped
3 tomatoes diced into cubes
3 cups diced brinjal
½ teaspoon chilli powder
½ teaspoon turmeric
Salt and pepper to taste

Method

Boil the onions and tomatoes in the water and then let it simmer for about 10 minutes. Add the rest of the ingredients and give it a stir. Cook for a further 20 minutes.

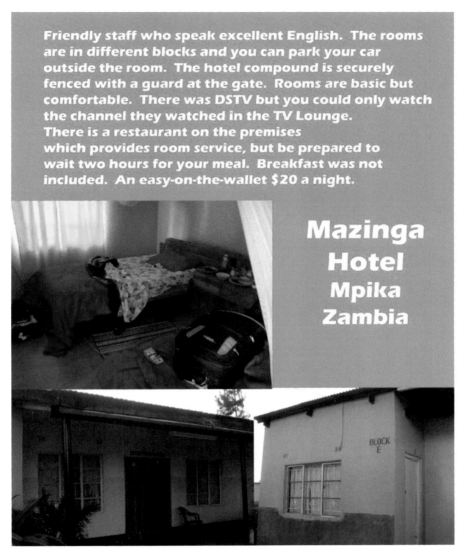

Friendly staff who speak excellent English. The rooms are in different blocks and you can park your car outside the room. The hotel compound is securely fenced with a guard at the gate. Rooms are basic but comfortable. There was DSTV but you could only watch the channel they watched in the TV Lounge.
There is a restaurant on the premises which provides room service, but be prepared to wait two hours for your meal. Breakfast was not included. An easy-on-the-wallet $20 a night.

Mazinga Hotel Mpika Zambia

Stats for the day					
Odometer Start	Odometer Finish	Day's Kilometres	Depart Time	Arrive Time	Hours travel
177 548	178 057	509	08h30	17h30	9 hours
Fuel	Cost local currency	Cost US$	Accommodation	Cost local currency	Cost US$
58.58 litres	50000TSH 270000 Kwacha	$85.85	Mazinga Hotel, Mpika	100000 Kwacha	$19.49

Day Four: Mpika to Lusaka

After a good night's sleep and a nice hot shower, we decided to get an early start and managed to get going at 7am, which was almost a record for us. This is where Siobhan and I do not have the same morning genes. I am a morning person, up bright and early ready to start my day. Siobhan on the other hand, will rather sleep until lunchtime and watch TV until 1am! We put in fuel at a nearby fuel station, topped up the water and gave Missy two cans of oil. She definitely runs better after an oil top-up; I'm not sure why seeing that I don't know too much about cars and their needs. We found a little bakery in Mpika which sold fresh bread rolls and not much else, and bought some to munch on for breakfast. Nothing like a dry bread roll and bottle of water to start your day! My brain cells were crying out for caffeine, but alas, no coffee seemed to be available anywhere.

While Siobhan watched a movie on my laptop the night before, I had pored over the newly purchased Zambia guide so that I could have a sense of where we were heading. Initially I had thought we could drive from Mpika all the way down to Livingstone, but after encountering the potholes the day before I decided that that was no longer on the cards. I don't think it's a good idea to drive the Zambian roads at night, especially if you are not too sure where you are headed. My years of doing all my driving during the night and resting during the day are long past. Now the old eyes don't see as well at night as they used to.

About 60km south of Mpika on the Great North Highway, you find a turn-off to the Nachikufu Cave. The guide book had said that it had some good San/Bushman rock paintings, so we thought we'd make a short detour and have a look. We were stopped at the turn-off by a man dressed in a suit, who informed us that he was the guide but he was going to Mpika so he couldn't show us the cave. Siobhan, the specialist of the disappointed look, managed to wordlessly convince him to let us see the cave without him. "Okay, my wife will be at my village. She can show you the cave as she has the keys."

Hmm, I wondered what kind of a cave it was that it had keys? We drove down a dirt road - one definitely needs a 4x4 - and found his wife outside his hut bending over a cooking fire. She explained that her husband wasn't there but then suggested that she hop into the car and show us the cave. We had to move stuff around on the back seat so she could squeeze in, and even so, when we went over a bump the cooler box slid down and hit her on the side of the head which she took in good spirit.

The setting for the cave was quite stunning. A fence had been erected around the cave site, as some very clever people had decided to write their names on the cave walls, over the San paintings. Obviously, they have a deep appreciation for the 15000 year old paintings! The paintings themselves were quite hard to see, having weathered and faded over the years. There was a small display with artefacts found at the site and also photos of the paintings when they were discovered in the 1940's. Those photos helped us to make out what we were supposed to be seeing. As San/Bushmen paintings go, they are probably not the best quality or best example, but it was still a pleasant enough detour and gave us a sense of how these early people lived. The cost to view the cave was a whopping 10 000 kwacha which converts to just under $2!

If we weren't two females on a mission to get down to Cape Town as quickly as possible, we would have spent a few days in the area, as there are cool waterfalls to check out, the Kasanka National Park, Shiwa Ng'andu Manor House and the Kapishya Hot Springs. Being a bit intrigued by David Livingstone as I've taught many classes about him over the years, I'd really have liked to make my way to Chitambo to stand on the spot where his heart was buried. Unfortunately, time didn't allow for it this visit, but I reckon we'll be back. This is the thing about exploring Africa, there is literally so much to see and do.

The next big town we were supposed to stop off at was Serenje. There is reportedly a fuel station there, but road signs are not a priority in Zambia, and the turn-off must have been there somewhere, but we missed it. Next thing we knew, we were in Mkushi, having completely by-passed Serenje without even noticing its existence. Mkushi is about 370km from Mpika. About the only sign of another vehicle we spotted on the highway was an overturned truck. The road was deserted, as if everybody had disappeared like those nuclear-war movies they had a few years back. One thing they do in both Zambia and in Tanzania, is put broken tree branches in the road to slow down traffic when there is a truck stuck on the road. I'm not sure why we need the road triangles if we can just use a machete to chop down tree branches which do the same thing.

Mkushi is just like a rural town in South Africa. We saw many farmers coming in for supplies and heard a lot of Afrikaans being spoken. We thought we were in the wrong country for a minute there! Talking about languages, the amazing thing about Zambia is that every single person speaks perfect English because that is the medium of instruction in all schools. With so many tribal languages, English was chosen as the main language, so you never have to worry about trying to communicate with people who can't speak English! Of course by the time we reached Mkushi, it goes without saying that our bladders were bursting. We stopped at a great little take-away called Shalom, which had tables outside you could sit at. They had a bathroom out back which was clean and had a flush toilet. The sausage roll and samosas we had were absolutely delicious and it was great to be able to leave the car for a while. Across the road from Shalom Take-away, was a fuel station where we could fill up.

From Mkushi, the next stop on the road to Lusaka is Kapiri Mposhi. The town is like a giant crossroads with main roads to other big towns leading off it in all directions. Kapiri Mposhi was the first time we encountered real traffic and there was definitely not going to be any more stopping to pee on the side of the road from here on. We stopped to buy giant lollipops to stuck on.

On the way to Kabwe, the next big town 60km south of Kapiri Mposhi and about 130km north of Lusaka, Siobhan decided to spit out of the window. Unfortunately, when a car is moving, spit can do strange things, and it was blown right back into her face. I struggled not to laugh as teenagers do not always find spit running down the side of their face very funny. But the moral of the story is and the life lesson Siobhan learnt was, "DO NOT SPIT OUT OF THE WINDOW OF A SPEEDING CAR."

After the spit incident, we tried to play Travel Scrabble which proved to be quite difficult with the constant swerving to avoid potholes. However, we soon worked out a system where Siobhan kept my letters, I just glanced at them and told her what to put down. It wasn't ideal as I couldn't really study the board to get maximum score as I had to keep my eyes on the road some of the time. Siobhan won but announced it to be a hollow victory as I wasn't giving the game my proper attention. Excuse me for not wanting to drive through potholes! Unfortunately, there were times when you couldn't avoid the potholes and it was about this time that my hazard lights came on indicating that a door was open. We stopped the car, opened and shut all the doors, banging then so hard that the car shook.

Poor Missy must have been wondering why we were punishing her! Of course with the boot lock broken, we couldn't open that, but despite our efforts the hazard lights kept flashing on and off intermittently whenever it chose. We couldn't figure out the pattern, or why they'd suddenly come on and then stop without us doing anything. It was most annoying. Almost as if the car was possessed!

Siobhan gave up on the Scrabble and started studying the guide to find a suitable place for us to stay for the night. Cairo Road in Lusaka seemed to be central with a large choice of accommodations to suit most budgets. However, Siobhan read that at night you are not advised to go out because of car hijackings. That made her eyes large and fearful. "I don't think we should stay in Lusaka, Mommy."

"Ah nonsense, it'll be okay," I said trying to make light of her concern. In truth I was a little worried myself. I had heard all these stories about Zambia, read other travellers' accounts on their blogs, yet so far had only met the nicest, friendliest people. Even the policemen who'd stopped us at the two road blocks we'd encountered had been friendly, only enquiring as to where we were going and wishing us a safe journey. None of the 'trying to find excuses to fine you' that we'd been told about. Nobody looked at our special red reflector stickers on the back bumper and white reflector stickers on the front bumper; or asked about the fire extinguishers, tow rope or special road triangles. We were so prepared and nobody was interested!

About 90km south of Kabwe, 40km north of Lusaka, we spotted a large signboard advertising the Protea Safari Lodge. A momentary feeling of generosity pulsed through my veins, and I suggested we see if they had any rooms. Protea Hotels are in my experience always of a good standard but also a little pricey. But I thought, what the heck, we'd been travelling for four days, stayed in adequate but not flash accommodation, why not treat ourselves a little? There was a time when we were on the 7km bumpy dirt road when I wondered if this was a good idea. However, when we reached the main gate I realised that it was a game lodge we were going to. We arrived at the reception at 4pm and felt as if we had stepped into another world – the world of the rich and famous. Opulent, luxurious, the Protea Safari Lodge is all that and more. Lush beautifully landscaped gardens, wildlife wandering around free between the thatched roof cottages; in all my life I had never encountered such luxury. The staff were friendly and very professional. $155 a night might sound pricey, but it was worth every cent! We were the only guests at the hotel, they were having a little down-time having just finished one conference group and were getting ready for the next to arrive in a few days.

Nothing was too much bother for the staff. As they'd just sprayed for mosquitoes in the dining lodge, they suggested we have room service instead of eating in the dining room. We ordered our meals – pepper fillet, t-bone steak, mushroom soup, sticky toffee pudding and at the exact time they said it would arrive, there was a knock at the door and a posse of waiters stood there carrying silver trays with our meals. The food was the best I'd eaten in I don't know how long. The bathroom, the size of my bedroom back home, had a large bath that you could relax in. I felt like a Hollywood star on safari.

After the most comfortable night's sleep ever, on pillows of the exact right softness, under a sumptuous duvet, we felt refreshed and ready to continue with our adventure. However, the Protea Safari Lodge had another surprise for us. A breakfast unlike any other breakfast we'd ever happened upon before. It didn't worry the Protea that we were the only guests; they laid out a breakfast buffet fit for a gathering of twenty heads of state. Fresh fruit, cheeses, cold meats, cereals, Danish pastries, muffins, croissants, a variety of breads, toast, juices and if that wasn't enough, they asked how we wanted our eggs and what we'd like with them. Siobhan was in seventh heaven. At last she had the eggs she'd been waiting for since Mbeya! I really cannot recommend this hotel highly enough; the excellent service, luxury, attention-to-detail, there is no way you can fault the Protea Safari Lodge. Forget about the money. Indulge yourselves. We did.

They have a wi-fi hotspot and went out of their way to get an adapter for my laptop as my power cable has a strange plug on the end. The manager came to chat with us, telling us a bit about the animals on the reserve, making us feel special, welcome, important. I think other hotels should take a leaf out of the Protea's book. Suffice it to say, we found it difficult to leave, eventually hitting the road at 12 noon. I decided to leave my sandals behind, as they fell apart when I walked back to our cottage from breakfast. It could have been because of the extra weight I was carrying after the enormous breakfast I'd consumed.

In 1993 on the 28th April, Zambia's entire 18-man **National Football Team** died in a tragic plane crash. The pilot was tired, having just returned from a flight to Mauritius the previous day, and accidentally switched off the still functioning right engine by mistake because of a "poor indicator light bulb" after the left engine failed, causing the plane to lose all power and crash. Altogether, thirty people died in the crash. The football team were supposedly the best on the continent at that time and were favoured to win the Africa Cup in 1994. To date, the Zambian National Football Team has never managed to achieve the successes of the team that perished in such a tragic accident.

Protea Safari Lodge
Lusaka Zambia

Pure luxury, we felt as if we were movie stars. Although we were the only guests at this 40-something room lodge, we were made to feel very welcome.
The rooms in chalets were tastefully decorated, no detail missed.

As if the rooms weren't beyond fantastic, the food was to die for. Perfectly grilled pepper fillet, sticky toffee pudding, we feasted like kings. The full English breakfast surpassed our wildest dreams and the wildlife wandering freely between the chalets made this a magical experience. A once-in-a-lifetime $155 a night.

Stats for the day					
Odometer Start	**Odometer Finish**	**Day's Kilometres**	**Depart Time**	**Arrive Time**	**Hours travel**
178 057	178 709	652	07h00	16h00	9 hours
Fuel	**Cost local currency**	**Cost US$**	**Accommodation**	**Cost local currency**	**Cost US$**
112.42 litres	880000 Kwacha	$171.54	Protea Safari Lodge, Lusaka	$155	$155

Day Five: Lusaka ▇▇ to Livingstone ▇▇

Zambia was proving to be an absolute delight. The people all spoke English, were friendly and helpful, Lusaka was very clean and modern. Even the cows you saw on the side of the road were twice as fat as the ones back in Tanzania. I think, that Zambia is a secret treasure. They have the same game in large parks that cost a fraction of what you are charged in Tanzania or South Africa; beautiful scenery, lovely waterfalls and bush walks. Zambia has the potential to become a top tourist destination.

The highway from Lusaka heading south to Livingstone was in mint condition with few if any potholes. The road was much busier than up north and there were large towns where one could stop to refuel should the need arise. Finding a toilet though, was a bit of a challenge. Siobhan had a desperate need, and my need though not quite as desperate, was starting to go that way. We pulled into Mazabuka and drove down to the large Shoprite Centre, convinced there'd be a toilet there. All those glasses of juice from breakfast and filter coffees were starting to take their toll. Alas, we encountered our first unfriendly person in Zambia. The toilets at the Shoprite Centre were not for customers, even if they had a desperate need. "That's okay then," I said with false cheer clamping my legs together, "We're not customers. We have no intention of buying anything from your Shoprite."

"It doesn't matter if you're a customer or not. They are only for staff. Find yourselves another toilet," the woman added nastily.

We crab-walked to the car in a strange scuttling gait, while we tried to keep our bladders from overflowing. By now I could hardly see out of my eyes as they were swimming in a sea of urine. "I have to go, I have to go," Siobhan kept repeating and I had to admit I was feeling the same way. I spotted a very shifty looking bar, and we decided to try there. Desperate times call for desperate measures, and I cursed that unfriendly woman at Shoprite who wouldn't share her toilet. Some shady characters at the bar directed us to some derelict stalls next to the building. Smelly urine-splattered squatter toilets, but we were so desperate we hardly noticed. As we were leaving, one of the shady characters shouted that we had to pay them money for using their toilets, but we just turned a deaf ear and walked even faster towards the car.

The rest of the trip went without incident; the three road blocks we went through were all friendly and I thought we'd easily make Livingstone before nightfall. Unfortunately, about 50km from Livingstone, the road changed from being a modern highway to a nightmare, which slowed us down considerably. Extensive roadworks were under way and we went through four different gravel road detours, where you could travel only between 20 and 30km an hour behind slow-moving trucks with dust blurring your vision. The parts of the highway between the detours were pure hell, with huge potholes making progress very slow. I think in one of the potholes I knocked something from my exhaust, as my car lacked power afterwards and sounded a little more like a tractor than a car. My hazard lights were on permanently now, which was okay because all the other cars and trucks also had their hazard lights on as vision was so difficult in all the dust that was churned up on the dirt roads.

Before dark descended upon us, Siobhan had been studying the travel guide and had picked out a Backpackers called The Fawlty Towers as a place we should stay. I must admit, the description sounded very appealing. Unfortunately, the directions in the guide book were a little off and we couldn't find it. By this time I needed a bathroom badly again, and we pulled into the first decent-looking guesthouse we saw. Luck wasn't on our side; they were full, but they did let me use their bathroom. There was quite a noisy bar next to the rooms, so it was probably a good thing we didn't get to stay there. By now it was 7pm. We drove around the block and saw signs for Chantler's Lodge. "Sounds expensive," Siobhan said with a worried look, trying to read the guide book in the dark.

Chantler's Lodge was a good find. The parking is safe and secure, with a high wall, big gate and 24-hour security guard. The accommodation is in small self-contained cottages and you can park in front of your cottage. $60 didn't seem a big price to pay for what we got. There is a restaurant where we probably had the best dinner of the whole trip. Deliciously tender and succulent pepper fillets and fresh chips. The owner of the lodge, Richard Chantler, came to chat to us and make sure that everything was alright. The personal interest he takes in his guests makes this lodge a cut above the rest. He had been the manager of the 4 star Ridgeway Hotel in Lusaka for 13 years and was something of an entertainment guru in his time. Although he's retired, he's obviously putting his experience to good use and the guesthouse he's set up in Livingstone is run very professionally, with good service being the key. The rooms were very comfortable and it didn't take much for us to fall asleep and have a good night's rest.

Livingstone gets its name from Scottish missionary and explorer, David Livingstone, who became the first European to see the **Victoria Falls** in 1855. The Victoria Falls is positioned halfway along the 2700km Zambezi River as it commences its journey from its source to the sea. The Victoria Falls, named after Queen Victoria, is 1700m wide and drops about 100m into the chasm below, making it the largest curtain of water in the world.

David Livingstone died from dysentery and malaria in the village of Chitambo in 1873. The local men traveling with him removed his heart and internal organs and buried them under a mupundu tree. They then salted and dried his body before disguising it in a tree, and then embarked on a nine month journey covering 1600km of bush to reach Bagamoyo on the Tanzanian coast. There they shipped Livingstone's preserved body to London, where he was finally buried in Westminster Abbey in April 1874.

It was good that the other places we tried were all full, otherwise we might have missed this little gem. Secure parking outside your self-contained bungalow with a 24-hour guard at the gate.

Chantler's Lodge
Livingstone Zambia

Staff speak excellent English. Comfortable rooms. Great restaurant. Full English breakfast included. Owner takes a personal interest in the guests. What more can you ask for? Good value at $60 a night.

Stats for the day					
Odometer Start	Odometer Finish	Day's Kilometres	Depart Time	Arrive Time	Hours travel
178 709	179 258	549	12h00	19h00	7 hours
Fuel	Cost local currency	Cost US$	Accommodation	Cost local currency	Cost US$
39.66 litres	300000 Kwacha	$58.48	Chantler's Lodge, Livingstone	$60	$60

BOTSWANA

Day Six: Livingstone ▮ I to Francistown ▬

We were up bright and early ready to go to the Victoria Falls before leaving Zambia. A full English breakfast was included at Chantler's Lodge and Siobhan got to have eggs again. While we were having breakfast, they washed our car which was covered under a thick layer of dust from the detours of the night before. We'd been to the Victoria Falls about thirteen years previously when Siobhan was about a year old. Obviously, she didn't remember anything from that visit. I did remember getting wet from the spray and ending up looking like a walking advert for a wet t-shirt competition.

The Victoria Falls are definitely one of nature's miracles and an absolute spectacle. They are just as good from the Zambian side as they were on the Zimbabwean side all those years ago. You pay $5 for the car, and entry to the park is $20 per person. Not wanting to travel in wet clothes, we paid the small fee to hire raincoats, which was just as well. The spray from the falls was unbelievable. We saw David Livingstone's statue there, with a football pushed under his foot. Further evidence that we were getting closer to the Football World Cup.

Siobhan of course, was completely fearless and hung over the edge of the railings. Being not so good with heights myself, I tried to stay away from the edge. Much to my chagrin, there was a small footbridge that stretched across the Zambezi Gorge. Of course Siobhan wanted to cross it, and of course she expected me to accompany her. Facing your fear is never easy, and without looking at the spectacular falls I managed to get across. My heart was beating in my ears and I thought I was going to throw up. I'm definitely not a candidate for bungee jumping!

It stands to reason, that if you go across the bridge, you have to walk over it to get back to the other side. I stood at the bridge and I knew that I couldn't do it again. There was no way in hell I could walk on a narrow slippery wooden bridge covered in green slime, that was suspended in the air so high above a gorge. I couldn't do it. No matter how much Siobhan cajoled me, my feet just wouldn't move. Eventually, I knew that I just had to do it. The only other way back to my car was if the SWAT team dropped down from a helicopter and lifted me up and carried me across, and realistically, that was not going to happen. I closed my eyes and hobbled across, gingerly putting down one foot in front of the other. About ten metres from the end I stopped. I couldn't do it, I couldn't step forward, I couldn't go backwards. I could feel a sob catch in my throat and I couldn't believe I was going to start crying. I'd rather face a herd of charging elephant than walk across that bridge. "Mom, you have to, there are people coming up behind us. You're blocking the bridge!" Siobhan was starting to sound anxious. My fear was no longer funny to her. I took a deep breath and clamped my eyes shut, Siobhan holding me from behind as we slowly made our way to the end of the bridge. I'll definitely visit the Victoria Falls again, but never will I set foot on that slippery footbridge. My heart won't take it.

39

The sheer volume of the water cascading down blows the mind. We decided to wander through the craft market at the Falls car park as we were trying to find an 'I Love Zambia' sticker. We needed to show our affection for this wonderful country and delightful people. (With the exception of the Shoprite lady of course!) Everybody wants you to inspect their wares, haggle over prices and buy from them. Tempting as it was, we were not in the market to buy as we knew we'd be returning to Tanzania with a heavily-laden vehicle.

Our negotiations to trade our cooler box with three apples and two juices included for an ornate wire earring tree, were interrupted by a baboon racing past us clutching some poor tourists' carrier bag with their Steers Take-away lunch in it. The tourists were running shouting after the baboon who hopped over the seven-foot fence with ease and sat on the other side pushing handfuls of hot Steers chips into its mouth while staring at the tourists who were waving their arms frantically on the other side of the fence. There was no way they'd get their lunch bag back. The baboon was taunting them, making fast work with its contents. Our negotiations concluded, we'd swopped our cooler box for a mask, an earring tree and a traditional doll; we started heading towards the mighty Zambezi River and the border with Botswana.

Despite being a vegetarian, the hippo is responsible for more human fatalities in Africa than any other animal. **Hippos** spend most of their day lolling about in water and can stay submerged for more than 10 minutes. If a small fishing boat or canoe filled with tourists happens to be above their heads when they come up for air, there's little to protect the vessel from the aggressive hippo. In March 2010, a US Marine on holiday made the news when he saved the life of a man who had a hippo charge his canoe and then chomp off his foot while kayaking on the Zambezi River.

We finally left Livingstone at 11am, after stopping off to buy some Steers for lunch later in the day. The baboon had whet our appetite! It was about an hour to the border and we were met with the border chaos that we were accustomed to. Touts waving fists of pula and dollars, agents wanting to assist you, everybody wanting to help for a price. Once again, we shooed away all the agents, but did change our remaining kwacha for pula, not

getting the best of

exchange rates, but not wanting to take a chance that we'd need pula on the other side and not be able to get it. Immigration and Customs were a doddle - just a stamp in the passport, only one wise-arse telling us we had to pay a $10 leaving tax, and we could give it to him to give to the police for us. We chose to ignore him, paid $25 for a ferry ticket to take our car across the Zambezi on the Kazangula ferry, and waited our turn in the queue of vehicles waiting to drive onto the ferry. There were no Customs or Immigration people manning the exit gate, nobody to check the car, nobody to officially wave you out of Zambia. As easy as a walk in the park.

The Botswana side was just as easy. Even though I pushed my car's papers towards them, the Customs were not interested at all in perusing them. They filled in a form, stamped it, I handed over 240 Pula which is about $35 for road tax and I was done. Easy as pie. There wasn't even anybody manning the gate to take the voucher from me. There was a strange man dressed like a cowboy who seemed out of place and near him a machine offering free condoms to all visitors to Botswana.

We had to drive through some special liquid to clean our tyres, part of their strict disease-control measures and we were on our way. Having lived in Botswana for four years quite some time ago, I was quite interested to see if it had changed in any way. The whole border crossing, Zambia to Botswana, waiting for the ferry and crossing the river had taken us only an hour-and-a-half!

We stopped at Nata, a small town in the middle of nowhere to refuel and use the bathroom. Unfortunately, the old lady sitting next to the toilets wanted a one pula coin from each person who used the toilet. As I know my own body quite well, I knew I had reached emergency status. I didn't have any pula coins on my person, not having had the opportunity to change money yet, but luckily a fellow visitor took pity on us (she must have seen the agonised looks on our faces) and gave me some pula coins to pay to the old lady so we could use the toilet.

From Nata to Francistown, not only did we pass miles and miles of sunflower farms, but we also spotted impala, a herd of kudu, two herds of springbok, warthogs, baboons and nine different sightings of elephant on the side of the road! The first time we saw elephant, we were so busy trying to get a good shot of them as they escaped into the bush, that we failed to notice a huge elephant watching us warily from the other side of the road. Then there was the elephant that was sleeping with its head resting against a tree, and another who came to the fence on the side of the road and carefully stepped over the fence as if it was hot coals.

The road seemed longer than I remembered; Francistown seemed further away. It could also be that I was just getting stressed with my hazard lights which were flicking on and off non-stop, like some sort of disco-vehicle heading off to a baboon bush party. Francistown didn't have many happy memories for me. It was where my marriage had irretrievably broken down. I don't know about you, but I associate places and songs with things that happened in my life. I did have happy memories staying at the Marang Hotel on the Tati River, so that was where I decided we would spend the night. I could remember my son and eldest daughter loving the chalets on stilts, like tree-houses around a beautiful park, and wanted Siobhan to have that same experience. After all, she was only about 18 months old when we had last stayed there.

Finding the Marang Hotel proved to be a mission in itself. Francistown no longer looked anything like I remembered it. The one horse in the one-horse town had been replaced with shopping malls, restaurants, building developments and many more streets. We found ourselves lost in the middle of a city which had blossomed in the thirteen years we'd been away, not sure which road or direction to take. To make matters worse, it was already 7.30pm and pitch dark. I was tempted to book into a Town Lodge which was across the road from a Spur Steak ranch, neither of which had been there thirteen years ago. However, I had made the mistake of building up the Marang Hotel to be something wonderful in Siobhan's mind; I could see that she was keen for us to try harder to find it. After asking several different people and getting several different directions, we finally found the Marang Hotel which is now owned by the Cresta Group. This means, that it is far more expensive than it used to be.

As I hopped down from the car, ready to go to the hotel's reception, gravity took control. I had not even thought about needing a toilet, the urge was simply not there, but standing up after being sitting for all those hours, my bladder protested. Violently. I had to use all my powers and muscles to clam those rusty old bladder valves shut - with the result, that I couldn't walk. Not a step. Siobhan did not understand my urgency, my inability to move. She shouted at me, tried to cajole me along, but to no avail A bell-hop from the hotel came to take our luggage, but I waved him away. We had only a small bag we could carry ourselves, and there was no way I was able to follow him anyway. I did try though, shuffling my feet forward, making sure I didn't separate my knees. I prayed that the people in the casino on the right could not witness my agonising walk.

Siobhan was losing her patience with me, as she also needed a bathroom. "Just go in the bushes," she hissed angrily. I thought of reminding her that if we'd just stayed at the Town Lodge we'd have relieved ourselves by now. It was her insistence that we find the Marang which was what had tried my bladder's patience. I couldn't go in the bushes, there were too many people coming in and out of the casino. With daughter leading the mother, we slowly made our way to the hotel reception, feeling a little out of place amongst all the rich folk hobnobbing there as the reception opened up into the dining area. Thank goodness I spotted a sign saying 'LADIES' on a door near the reception area.

The price of the Marang Hotel had increased in the same proportion over the last thirteen years, as the amount of shopping malls in Francistown. Siobhan's eyes grew big when she heard the price, forgetting all about my wet patch. "It's okay. I'm tired and I need a bath. Let's just do it." I smiled and tried to give Siobhan a hug. She moved away, still annoyed with me.

"866 Pula per person, but I won't charge for your daughter as she was born here. Would you be having breakfast?"

"Is it included?" I asked hopefully as we were shelling out a lot more money for a room than I'd budgeted for.

"I'm afraid not. It's an extra hundred and..."

I was rude. I didn't even let her finish. "No thanks. We'll find something cheaper along the road."

A deaf bell-hop used sign language to communicate with us, and indicated that we should get back into our car and drive behind him as he showed us the way to our chalet on stilts. That was just as I had remembered it! The chalet was luxurious, maybe not quite up to the standard of the Protea Safari Lodge, but close. We ordered steak and chips through room service and then I drew a nice hot bath. The food took ages to come. Maybe they had to slaughter the beast first to get the steak, or go out into the fields to dig up the potatoes they needed for the chips; but regardless, the wait was unacceptable. Siobhan called room service a few times to find out what had happened to our food. Eventually, when we were both about to nod off to sleep, the food arrived and they had cocked up the order! Not only did we get our steak and chips, but we also got a portion of fish and chips. "We didn't order that," I said pointing to the large plate filled with a generous helping of fried fish and chips. The room service waitress just shrugged her shoulders and left the plate of fish and chips there, but didn't charge us for it. Unfortunately, she didn't leave a bottle opener, so I was unable to open up the bottle of apple cider I'd ordered, which was very annoying.

Francistown was the site of Southern Africa's first 'Gold Rush' when gold prospector, Karl Mauch, found gold in 1867 along the Tati River. The Francistown area still has old and abandoned mines.

Beautiful location on the banks of the Tati River. You can stay in a room, chalet on stilts or camp in the lush gardens. Very kid-friendly, not only has a great playground, but chalets have a special room for kids complete with fold-out beds. The restaurant is good but pricey and tariff does NOT include breakfast. A bit of a rip off considering the cost of a chalet at $122 per person per night. Luckily Siobhan was free because she was born in Botswana!

Marang Hotel Francistown Botswana

Stats for the day					
Odometer Start	Odometer Finish	Day's Kilometres	Depart Time	Arrive Time	Hours travel
179 258	179 865	607	11h00	19h30	8 and a half hours
Fuel	Cost local currency	Cost US$	Accommodation	Cost local currency	Cost US$
78.7 litres	300000 Kwacha 260 Pula	$95.31	Marang Hotel, Francistown	866 Pula	$122.66

SOUTH AFRICA

If Francistown had looked different to what I'd remembered at night, in daylight it was completely unrecognisable. We found a shopping mall with a fuel station, *bureau de change* and Wimpy attached. Everything we needed. Wimpy is famous for its good value-for-money breakfasts, and you didn't have to twist our arm to get us in there for eggs and bacon! The bonus is, besides a good breakfast you pay $10 less per person than the Marang wanted to charge for the morning munch. Although we had a long drive ahead, we weren't in a big hurry, so we savoured our meal, enjoyed our coffee, changed dollars for pula, filled the car with petrol and finally left Francistown at 10am.

Along the highway, there are disease control stops where you have to drive through some special stuff. Cattle farming is big business in Botswana as they supply the European Union countries with beef. That's why they are so concerned about keeping their cattle safe from Foot and Mouth Disease. Somewhere along the highway, one of these disease control stops appeared on the horizon manned by traffic police determined to make their annual quota in one day. Either that or pay for their daughter's wedding! I slowed down as I saw the stop sign ahead. About three metres behind that stop sign was another stop sign with the barrier. As the stop signs were so close together, I took the first one to be a slow down one, and the second one to be the one you actually stopped at. The policeman was waiting there with a psychotic smile on his face, anticipating drivers to make that exact mistake. He stopped the woman in front of me, myself and as I had to pull off the road, I saw he stopped the man in the car behind me. All of us had committed the same crime. Failing to stop completely at the first stop sign. He decided to deal with the other drivers first, speaking rapidly in Setswana and gesticulating wildly with his hands. He wrote up fines for them and sent them on their way, then turned to me, evil dripping from his smile. "You have a foreign car, so 1000 Pula spot fine. You failed to stop at the first stop sign."

I gasped and could feel my delicious Wimpy breakfast rise in my throat. It would serve the bastard right if I vomited it up on his shiny black shoes. "You can't be serious," I stammered.

"I am very serious. 1000 Pula spot fine for your transgression," he said in perfect English.

I quickly calculated that in my head. Over $100, this guy was just chancing his luck. "It's illegal to have two stop signs so close together. You've done that deliberately just to catch people. That is corrupt and I'll have to report you." Of course, I had no idea whether or not having two stop signs so close to each other was illegal. But I did make the police guy think about his spot fine.

"Okay, you can go this time. I'll let you off. But next time stop at the first stop sign." He waved us away and walked to his post, ready to catch the next driver.

At Pahalapye, a small town that hadn't changed much in the thirteen years since I'd last stopped there, we decided we needed to find a bathroom urgently. Memories of the night before's toilet stop was still fresh in our minds. The Wimpy coffee is delicious, but it does go right through your system quite quickly. Two cups of Wimpy coffee were now knocking at the door ready to come out. We stopped at a small shopping mall with a fuel station, convinced they'd have a toilet, which indeed they had. Unfortunately, the woman sitting outside the bathroom collecting pula for its use was blocking the entrance. "You can't go in," she said, "Toilet not working. No water."

By now both Siobhan and I were walking like scuttling crabs each missing three legs. "You can't be serious," I gasped feeling my eyeballs start to float, "Is there another toilet here somewhere?"

"There," she said, pointing in the direction of Chicken Licken.

"Cool, Chicken Licken, just what I feel like," said Siobhan, her eyes lighting up. You need to know that Siobhan has this thing for Fast Food; a perpetual craving. At various stages of the trip up until that point, she'd expressed her desire to feast at Macdonalds, Nandos chicken, Kentucky Fried Chicken, Wimpy, Spur Steak ranch and of course Chicken Licken. "I can't wait to get to Cape Town and go to..." and then she'd name some of the Fast Food chains. With my need for a toilet escalating at each passing minute, the last thing I felt like was eating Chicken Licken or anything else for that matter.

"Let's keep our mind focused and find a toilet," I snarled as I walked at a furious pace in the direction of Chicken Licken.

"Sorry, no toilet here. Try the Engen," the plump woman in the tight-fitting Chicken Licken uniform pointed us in the direction from which we'd come.

"Mom, can we..." Siobhan was salivating at the pictures of the fried chicken meals displayed on the wall.

"Later. Toilet first," I said, sweat now starting to form on my brow from the exertion of keeping the bladder valve shut. We walked briskly back to the Engen toilet at the fuel station.

"Welcome," the woman said, allowing us to enter the bathroom. The same woman who had blocked the entrance five minutes before saying the toilet was broken and that there was no water. The toilets were in working order, clean and there definitely was water. So I'm not sure why that woman felt the need to put us through all that agony. Feeling much lighter, we skipped across the parking lot to Chicken Licken and bought fried chicken and chips for lunch.

We arrived in Gaborone just after 3pm and I was amazed at how Gaborone had developed. It had always been a big city, but now I could see many new shopping malls lining the sides of the highway. We stopped at an Engen One Stop, went to the toilet even though the need wasn't great, definitely not wanting to repeat our Pahalapye episode later on in the afternoon, needing a toilet when there was none available.

RECIPES FROM AFRICA - **Botswana**

Seswaa
A different way of presenting meat and great for developing biceps. Make sure you have a meat mallet handy. This serves 6 and is eaten with rice or maize meal porridge and morogo.

Ingredients
1kg brisket
Water
1 large onion coarsely chopped
Salt and pepper to taste

Method
Place all ingredients in the water and boil for about 2 and a half hours until the meat is soft. Keep checking that you have water in your pan so you don't cremate your brisket. Drain the liquid into a cup. You can use this to make a gravy later. Get the meat mallet and pound the life out of the cooked brisket, until either you get a cramp in your bicep or the meat becomes flaky. Remove the bones as they reveal themselves. The dish is ready to serve.

Morogo
You'll find that all over Africa they make similar dishes to the Botswana Morogo, but they use leaves from different plants. In Botswana they tend to use sun-dried bean leaves, in Zambia leaves from the sweet potato plant, in Tanzania leaves from some wild plant called mchicha which I always thought was spinach but apparently it's not. So if you grow your own vegetables, you can experiment with the plant leaves to make your own Morogo, otherwise just use spinach leaves.

Ingredients
1kg chopped leaves
2 onions coarsely chopped
½ cup water
1 tablespoon cooking oil
Salt and pepper to taste

Method
Place the chopped leaves and chopped onion into a saucepan. Add the water and cooking oil. Boil for 15 minutes, taking care to stir continuously. Season with salt and pepper and it's ready to serve.

South Africa was so close now. I'd decided to enter South Africa through the border post at Lobatse, just 70km south of Gaborone. My reasons for choosing the Lobatse border rather than the Mmabatho one south of Lobatse was that it was much smaller. Although the Mmabatho one was on our direct route and exiting through Lobatse would mean us making a detour, my memories of the Mmabatho one was of lots of trucks going through and highly efficient staff. A much busier border. Definitely not what I needed. I wanted a more laidback border post manned by staff not quite as efficient. I'd been told that to enter South Africa with a foreign-registered car from a country not part of the SADC, I'd need a Carnet de Passage which you could only purchase for thousands of rands from the Automobile Association. Getting this Carnet was quite a complicated procedure. You had to apply online to the AA in South Africa, then arrange a bank transfer to deposit money into their account, then organise and pay for DHL to collect the Carnet and deliver it to you in the country you were residing in. As I said, a very complicated and costly exercise. One which I decided to chance my luck and forgo. With the result, when we reached Gaborone my nerves started to bounce up and down in anticipation of the border crossing. Even Siobhan practising her French accent and singing every sign post in opera didn't distract me from my visions of being refused entry into South Africa as I didn't have the required Carnet.

The hazard lights going on and off were really starting to annoy me, and we accidentally discovered that if we opened Siobhan's window, then the hazard lights would go off. As it turned out later, this was just a coincidence, but it did mean we could drive from Gaborone to Lobatse without the hazard lights going on.

The hills around **Lobatse** are the subject of many legends. The most famous one is the legend of Lover's Hill 15km from Lobatse at the village of Otse. Apparently, like in Romeo and Juliet, two lovers from rival families were denied permission to marry. They decided to elope and fled up the hill where they completely disappeared, never to be seen again. Legend has it that lovers climbing the hill will disappear. So if you are travelling with your lover, don't stop to climb the hill at Otse!

The tiny towns between Gaborone and Lobatse looked exactly the same as they did thirteen years earlier and even Lobatse hadn't changed much. I did make a small detour to show Siobhan the school I'd taught at when we lived there, and that had changed somewhat, with more classrooms and a high school. We drove through the town and I recognised some of the shops we used to frequent when we lived there. We arrived at the border post at 4.30pm and went through the Botswana side very quickly without any problems at all. They just waved us through, not even interested in checking our car. My stomach was tied up in knots when we arrived at the South African side though, as I was really worried about our lack of the required paperwork.

All my worrying and anxious moments were for nought, as the South African side just stamped our passports and Customs just stamped our exit pass. The guy in charge there was lolling back in his chair talking to another policeman about the football. Nobody asked to see my car's papers which I had ready, the Carnet or even picked up the fact that the car was foreign-registered. It was an anti-climax to end all anti-climaxes! However, at the exit gate there were policemen who checked the vehicle - the first vehicle check we'd encountered at any of the border posts we'd travelled through on the trip. They examined the jerry can to see that it wasn't carrying explosives and immediately pounced on the packet of pirate DVDs we'd bought in Iringa in Tanzania, which they wanted to confiscate. I begged and pleaded, Siobhan made her eyes go all watery, and when the police officer didn't see any movie he particularly wanted to watch, he let us keep them but gave us a warning not to buy pirate DVDs in future. Luckily, the pirate DVDs had distracted him from searching the car any further and discovering the tazer gun we had, as I'm not sure if that is legal in South Africa! The whole border crossing, both the Botswana and South African sides together, had taken us a total of 30 minutes!

Siobhan quickly put the DVD packet into the suitcase and we high-fived each other as we headed in the direction of Zeerust. Our celebrations were a bit early, as 10km from the border post we were stopped by policemen at a road block. They asked to look in our bags and suitcases, but wanted to see our passports first. I knew if they looked in our suitcase they'd find the packet of DVDs Siobhan had hidden in there. Luckily, the officer was so fascinated with all the stamps in our passport, that we managed to distract him and chat about travel and all the places we'd visited, that he forgot to look in our bags. He wished us a safe trip and waved us on. Our hazard lights started up again, and just outside Zeerust a traffic cop pulled us over. I prayed that I wasn't being stopped for speeding or any other problem with the car, as all I wanted now was to find a place to stay for the night. The traffic cop had only stopped us because he was concerned we had a problem with the car as the hazard lights were on. I explained that there must be a short or something and that we would get it sorted by an auto-electrician the next day. He wished us a safe trip and told us to take care.

We arrived at Zeerust at 6pm and stopped at Sha-henne's Guest House on the outskirts of the town. It was off the road with secure parking and the rooms were fully self-contained complete with small kitchen and cooking facilities. Sha-henne also had a Sports Bar and Steakhouse attached to the reception. As we didn't have much Rand, we decided to head into town and have a burger at the Wimpy for dinner. Zeerust had a new shopping mall since I'd been there last, but otherwise looked much the same as it had thirteen years ago. With jubilation, Siobhan and I toasted our safe arrival in South Africa with chocolate milkshakes. I still couldn't believe we'd managed to get into South Africa without that Carnet de Passage!

RECIPES FROM AFRICA - South Africa

Inkukhu Nembotyi

This dish is traditionally served with umngqusho, which is broken or stamped corn kernels mixed with an equally amount of sugar beans. The stamped corn kernels are called samp. While umngqusho is tasty, it is a mission to cook, and frankly I never have the time. The samp and beans have to be soaked overnight and then boiled and left to simmer for two hours. So, if you have time constraints like me, serve with rice or maize meal porridge. This dish serves 4-6.

Ingredients

2 cups cooking oil
1 onion finely sliced
3 deboned chicken breasts cut into strips
1 teaspoon ginger
1 teaspoon garlic powder
1 teaspoon masala
1 cup green beans
1 cup chicken stock
Salt and pepper to taste

Method

1. Heat the oil and fry the onion until golden brown.
2. Add the chicken strips and fry until soft.
3. Add seasonings and spices.
4. Add the whole green beans and chicken stock.
5. Simmer gently until cooked through.

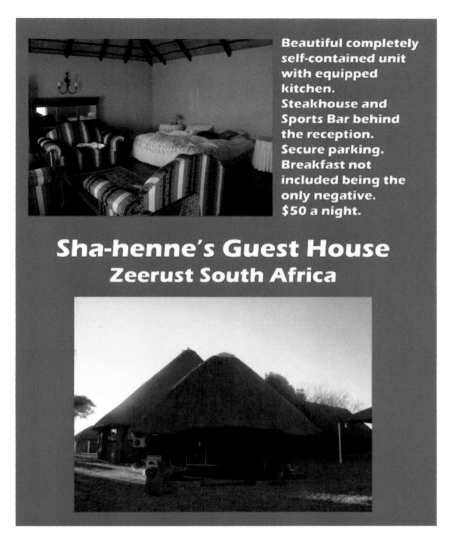

Beautiful completely self-contained unit with equipped kitchen. Steakhouse and Sports Bar behind the reception. Secure parking. Breakfast not included being the only negative. $50 a night.

Sha-henne's Guest House
Zeerust South Africa

Stats for the day					
Odometer Start	**Odometer Finish**	**Day's Kilometres**	**Depart Time**	**Arrive Time**	**Hours travel**
179 865	180 473	608	10h00	18h00	8 hours
Fuel	**Cost local currency**	**Cost US$**	**Accommodation**	**Cost local currency**	**Cost US$**
96.7 litres	600 Pula	$84.99	Sha-henne's Guest House, Zeerust	R390	$50.72

After a great night's sleep we woke up refreshed and ready to continue with our journey to Cape Town. There were just a few things we had to do first, like get the hazard lights sorted, buy a South African simcard for the cellphone, have breakfast and change Dollars for Rands. The first thing was obviously to get some cash , as without any Rands we couldn't do any of the other things on our list. Getting money proved to be a mission and a half! ABSA Bank did not do currency exchanges on a Saturday and they sent us to First National Bank. First National Bank would not change Dollars for South African citizens who did not have an account with them. So, basically we were screwed. The bank teller then suggested we go to a Bureau de Change on the road to the Botswana border, one which the truck drivers use. We found the pink building the teller had described in the middle of nowhere. I'd be nervous working there so isolated, handling all that money, if I was the staff. We managed to change our Dollars into Rands and get a good exchange rate. I mentioned the isolation of the Bureau de Change to the woman working there behind bullet-proof glass, and asked if she wasn't afraid to be there alone. She told us that the Saturday before, the other woman who worked there was shot in a hold up and was still in hospital. We couldn't leave there fast enough, terrified that we'd be caught in another armed robbery.

Our next stop was at an auto-electrician. This proved to be another mission. The one was closed, the other had gone out of business and the third was based at a mechanic shop. The mechanics were all there but the auto-electrician had taken the day off. I was not sure if we'd be able to continue driving with our hazard light problem as we seemed to be attracting a lot of attention from police and other motorists. The chief mechanic directed us to a car spares shop where one of the guys who worked there could do auto-electrical jobs. We found his shop next to the Wimpy, and he checked out the car. The solution to our problem was far simpler than I could ever have comprehended. In fact, I actually felt a little stupid when he repaired it for no cost. It wasn't Siobhan's door which was the problem, so our thinking that if we opened her window the hazard lights would stop flicking was just a bizarre coincidence when that worked. It was my door which was the problem. All that it was, was that the special detector on the door was no longer making contact when the door was closed. All the auto-electrician did was put a piece of tape on the special detector so that it made contact when the door was closed. It took two minutes to find a solution to a problem that had driven us crazy for several days!

It was amazing how much the temperature had dropped the further south we drove. We had definitely gone from endless summer to a cold winter and realised that we were hopelessly under-dressed. So after another great Wimpy breakfast, we found a clothing store and stocked up on some warm clothes for our last two days of driving before reaching Cape Town and our winter clothes which were in storage there. We finally left Zeerust at 10.45am, not sure where we would be spending the next night, only knowing that we were getting ever closer to our destination and we would drive until it got dark.

We were stopped for speeding just out of Mafikeng, by a traffic cop holding a speed camera. After noticing our foreign registration, he asked if we were visiting South Africa for the Football World Cup obviously assuming we were foreign tourists. Although South Africans, we thought it best to go along with his 'foreign tourist' theory, and nodded our heads, too afraid to speak in case he picked up our South African accents. He wished us a safe journey, told us to enjoy the beautiful country, and we sped off.

Mafikeng has a bit of an interesting history. On the 29th December 1895, Leander Starr Jameson together with 600 men, most of whom were Matabeleland policemen, left from near Mafikeng to launch an attack on Paul Kruger's Transvaal Republic. The intention was to seize the Boer armoury in Pretoria and restore order amongst the angry British expats who were working on the goldmines in Johannesburg. Cecil John Rhodes, who was governor of the Cape Colony at the time, had reputedly initiated the raid, as he had his eyes set on the rich goldfields of the Transvaal. Jameson's party had stupidly cut the telegraph lines to Cape Town and not the lines to Pretoria, so the Boers were informed of the impending attack and were lying in wait for them when they arrived. The Jameson Raid ended Rhode's career as governor, he lost credibility with the British Government and Jameson and the survivors of the raid were all arrested and handed back to Britain to face trial. The media used the Raid to whip up anti-Boer feeling amongst the public. The Transvaal Republic was paid a million pounds in compensation by the British South Africa Company. After the Raid, the Boers began to amass weapons and this definitely was one of the causes of the Anglo-Boer war.

The Anglo-Boer War broke out four years after the Raid in 1899. The British decided that defence was the best form of attack and made a stand at Mafikeng because of its close proximity to the border of the Transvaal Republic. The Siege of Mafikeng lasted from 13 October 1899 to 17 May 1900. Lord Baden-Powell, the British commander at Mafikeng used innovative ideas like fake landmines, a train filled with sharpshooter sent into the Boer Camp, and a cadet corps made up of 12-15 year old boys to act as scouts and messengers, to keep the Boer forces at bay. After 217 days, the Boers retreated and gave up on the attack and rather utilised their men elsewhere. The cadet corps inspired Baden-Powell to start the Boy Scout Movement which is still around today.

By lunch time our stomachs were grumbling, and when we drove into Vryburg we started singing when we saw signs on the road for a Spur Steak Ranch. Every large town in South Africa has a Spur Steak Ranch, and it has become something of a tradition amongst South African families. We parked our car outside the Spur and an old white man came to ask if he could guard our car for a tip. That is definitely a sign of how times have changed, as twenty years ago that would never have happened.

Vryburg was also the site of one of the concentration camps started by the British to incarcerate Boer women and children, as well as farm workers, when they were forcibly removed from their farms during the Scorched Earth Policy in the Anglo-Boer War. As they were losing the war against the Boers, the British resorted to desperate measures. They figured, if they could cut off the Boer's food supplies, they could starve them into submission. So, they burned down all farmhouses and fields of crops they encountered, and slaughtered all livestock leaving them to rot on the ground. Women, children and farm workers were rounded up and put into camps which had appalling conditions. Altogether, 27 000 women and children and close on 15 000 farm workers and their families died of starvation and disease in the camps.

10km South of Vryburg in the middle of nowhere is Tiger Kloof. The London Missionary Society bought the Tiger Kloof farm in the early 1900s. In 1904, Mr Willoughby, arrived with a wagon, a tent and a few tools. His task was to be the first principal of the Tiger Kloof School he had yet to build. The goals of Tiger Kloof were to excel at both academic and commercial training, and in fact, the school was built by the boys studying to be builders there. One of the most famous students to attend Tiger Kloof, was Sir Seretse Khama who became the first black president of Botswana.

Between Vryburg and Kimberley is Taung. Taung is a small town that is so tiny you might not even realise you've driven through it. What makes it worth mentioning, is the discovery of a skull of a 3 year old child in 1924. It was the first hominid skull to be discovered in Africa, and was later names Australopithecus Africanus. The marks on the skull suggest the child was killed and eaten by a large bird of prey.

Our bellies full, it was time to hit the road again. I was still toying with the idea of perhaps driving through the night to get to Cape Town. You know what it's like, when you're so close to your destination, you just want to get there. I had travelled that road many times in the past usually at night as it was so boring to drive it during the day. Reason did take over. When I'd driven that route during the night I'd been much younger and had quite good night vision. These days I'm an old woman who is virtually night blind, so it probably wouldn't be a good idea to attempt a night-drive. We reached Kimberly at 5pm, filled the car with fuel, used the bathroom and bought KFC for dinner. I was starting to get sick of chips and fast food and was missing the beef stew and nshima I'd had in Zambia. Kimberly is a very interesting town, and I'd be lying if I didn't admit that I was sorely tempted to spend the night in Kimberly and explore the town with Siobhan the next morning. Unfortunately, the cords tying me to Table Mountain were pulling me ever harder, and I was unable to resist, so I just stared longingly at the Formule One Hotel as we drove past heading out on the highway to the next town. We drove past signs advertising the Big Hole and the Battlefield Route, and continued on the road, dusk fast approaching.

The Big Hole in Kimberley is an open-pit diamond mine which is claimed to be the largest hole in the ground excavated by hand. From July 1871 to 1914, 50 000 miners dug the hole with picks and shovels. All in all, they collectively gathered 2720kg of diamonds.

Besides its richness in diamonds, **Kimberley** also achieved fame during the 124 day siege of Kimberley in the Anglo-Boer War which began in earnest on the 6th November 1899. The Boers surrounded the town and thought they'd force the inhabitants to capitulate by shelling the town at random intervals and preventing food and supplies from reaching the town. However, the town's inhabitants stood firm and held out until relief arrived, sometimes even taking cover down the Kimberley Mine.

Crossing the Orange River

Battle of Magersfontein on 11 December 1899. Near Kimberley lies the hill of Magersfontein where the British suffered one of their biggest defeats during the Anglo-Boer War. Anticipating the arrival of British Troops to relieve the Siege of Kimberley, Boer forces dug trenches at the foot of the Magersfontein Hill. The British duly arrived and started shelling the top of the hill where they thought the Boers were hiding. When the British followed their shelling with a charge, they were gunned down by the Boers hiding in the trenches. The Boers had a total force of 8500 men compared to the 15 000 trained British soldiers. One would have expected the British to easily defeat the Boers. Altogether, 948 British soldiers were killed and wounded compared to 236 from the Boers.

It was pitch dark, Missy's brights already on when we drove into Hopetown. Although there were quite a few signs for different guesthouses, when we knocked on doors or rang bells there was no reply. It seemed either there was a big party on in town which everybody had gone to leaving the streets deserted, or guesthouse owners didn't really want the business. We drove until we found a restaurant/pub and asked them about accommodation in the town. The bartender explained that the only hotel had recently closed down and directed us to another guesthouse. Once again, no reply and no answer when I called the cell number displayed on a sign on the gate. This was getting ridiculous, and it was starting to look as if we'd have to keep on driving to Britstown, which is not what I wanted to do. As we were driving out of the town past the prison to get back up to the highway, we passed another sign for a guesthouse which we had missed when we'd driven into town. "Last try," I mumbled, "Can't believe people in this town don't want our business."

Words can't describe the relief we felt when at last someone answered our knock. The Hopetown Guesthouse was probably not the cheapest, but it was tastefully decorated with a small kitchen with tea and coffee supplied, and ample warm bedding for the freezing cold winter

 Hopetown nights. Apparently the morning before we arrived they'd had a black frost which killed many of the plants in the garden. The only disconcerting part about the room was the design which I felt was a little flawed. There was a shoulder-high brick wall which separated the toilet area from the bedroom, which meant that a person in the bedroom could clearly hear all private bathroom noises, and when you stood up in the bathroom, the person in the bedroom could see your head. This might not bother some people, but I did find it a bit off-putting.

The first diamond found in South Africa, was the 23.25 carat Eureka, found on a farm in **Hopetown**. Soon after the 83.5 carat Star of Africa was found, and this sparked the Diamond Rush. When the diamonds ran out in Hopetown, in 1897 a disgruntled local farmer decided breathe life back into the deserted town. He claimed to have experienced magnificent new finds on his farm and within three weeks 10 000 men rushed back to Hopetown. This second boom didn't last long. His sham was soon uncovered. This became known as "The Great Sucker Rush".

Hopetown Guest House
Hopetown South Africa

The only guest house in Hopetown actually wanting to do business. Nobody answered the door or phone of the other guest houses we tried.
Very comfortable room tastefully decorated.
There is tea, coffee, a fridge and a kettle, as well as DSTV. No meals or breakfast available.
The low wall separating the toilet from the bedroom doesn't allow for any privacy.
$59 a night.

Stats for the day					
Odometer Start	**Odometer Finish**	**Day's Kilometres**	**Depart Time**	**Arrive Time**	**Hours travel**
180 473	181 060	587	10h45	19h45	9 hours
Fuel	**Cost local currency**	**Cost US$**	**Accommodation**	**Cost local currency**	**Cost US$**
144.18 litres	R1213	$157.74	Hopetown Guest House	R450	$58.52

My body had forgotten how to handle extreme cold. During the night it was okay, as two thick duvets kept one warm and snug. However, at 6am as we shivered our way to the car to resume our journey, I thought I might freeze to death. It was only -1 degrees Celsius. Nothing compared to the -36 degrees Celsius we'd experienced during the day at Haerbin on the border of China and Siberia when we'd gone to view the Ice Festival there. This Hopetown cold should have been nothing for us, but it wasn't. We put on all three of our jumpers we had with us, and wrapped ourselves in the Maasai blankets we'd brought along, but still we froze. I knew that somewhere in my running shoes were feet with toes, but I'd lost all sensation in my extremities. I couldn't wrap the blanket around my feet as my car was a manual and I needed to be able to use the pedals. I know what you are thinking. Why doesn't the silly woman turn on the car's heater? Well, in Tanzania it is always warm so you never need to use the heater. The truth is, both Siobhan and I had no idea how to work the heater. Whatever button we pressed just seemed to blow out cold air and we decided to rather keep our frozen hands under the blankets than persist in pressing random buttons.

Progress was slow because of the many roadwork stops we encountered; some of the stops we had to wait half an hour before we were allowed to proceed, but it gave us time to enjoy the stunning sunrise. I was quite impressed that the roadwork crew used solar panels to produce the power needed to work the traffic lights at each detour.

The Karoo is not the most exciting of areas to travel through; you almost get excited when you see a couple of sheep grazing next to a fence. However, the vast emptiness, although desolate, is quite serene. So serene in fact, that it has lulled many motorists to sleep. The road has a reputation for being quite dangerous, the monotony of it being many a driver's undoing. The good news was that we managed to pick up a radio signal. After listening to the same music CDs over and over again, we knew all the songs by heart. In life there is always a balance, so it goes without saying that there had to be some bad news. In this case, the bad news was twofold. No, make that threefold. We could pick up only two radio

stations, one playing some strange church music that made us think we'd gone through a wormhole and travelled back 300 years in time; and the other a news station repeating the same news broadcast every thirty minutes. But the most important bit of bad news was that none of the small towns and hamlets we drove through had a coffee shop. All we wanted was a hot cup of coffee and a cup of hot chocolate to warm us up. Even with the sun out it wasn't warming up the inside of the car which was like the inside of a cold room at an abattoir. So my tip for you is this, if you are making this journey in winter, have a flask with you that you can fill with hot liquid of some kind. Even a bottle of brandy would have done the trick. As tempting as the brandy might be, forget I mentioned it. Drinking alcohol and driving do not go hand in hand.

Siobhan had been brewing a cold for a couple of days, and somewhere on the road to Three Sisters, a town named after the three koppies (hills) on its outskirts, it hit with a vengeance. Tired of blowing her nose, she stuck wads of toilet paper up each nostril, doing a damn good impersonation of a walrus which was quite distracting for me. Especially seeing that every time she spoke her tusks fluttered in the breeze of her breath. With road signs advertising an Ultra City ahead, we knew that we'd be able to finally get something hot to drink.

We rolled into Three Sisters at 9.45am, only just getting the feeling back in our toes, filled up the fuel tank and had a delicious Steers breakfast which was just what we needed at the time. A much-needed toilet-break, and we were back on the road at 10.40am, ready for the last part of our drive to Cape Town. I couldn't wait for my first view of Table Mountain. I knew though, that we still had a long boring road ahead of us. Siobhan resumed with her fascination with her body parts she'd started earlier on in the trip, using all the camera's battery power to take shots of herself. Which was annoying as my camera wasn't as good as the one she was using, but at least it kept her entertained.

 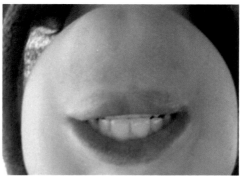

Cape Town was only 400km away and when we drove through Beaufort West, we didn't want to stop for lunch. Our prize was so close it was tangible. My son who was waiting for us in Cape Town, started texting us every half an hour to check our progress. As the landscape changed and the hills became greener and vineyards started appearing, we knew we were inching ever closer. Surrounding mountains were covered in a dusting of snow. Laingsburg also has an Ultra City and an Engen One Stop. You know that at those fuel stations you are guaranteed to find good clean toilets and a fast food restaurant, so that not only your car will get topped up.

On the outskirts of **Beaufort West** lies the 75 000 ha Karoo National Park. On 12 August 1883, the quagga, became extinct when the last mare of the species died in Amsterdam Zoo. The quagga is again roaming free in the park. It was recreated from portions of its genetic code present in tissue samples taken from a mounted museum exhibit.

On the 25th January 1981, the town of **Laingsburg** was completely devastated by a flood when the Buffels River burst its banks and submerged much of the town under water. 104 People lost their lives in the flood and only 21 houses were left standing. It is said that about 12 people were washed downstream and eventually rescued at the Floriskraal dam about 21km`s outside town.

There are no words to describe the feeling die-hard Capetonians feel when they set eyes on Table Mountain for the first time after being away for a year or more. It grips your soul and makes your eyes fill with tears. That mountain is some kind of symbol to me and I carry it in my heart. I am only ever truly home when I can look up and see my mountain. As spectacular as Mount Kilimanjaro might be, it just doesn't do it for me quite like Table Mountain does. When we reached Worcester in the valley of the mountains separating it from the Cape, I could almost smell the sea air. Then it was just the Du

Toit's Kloof Tunnel separating us from my mountain. As we came out of the tunnel and drove round the bend, Table Mountain rose majestically out of the haze.

For me it will always be one of the most awesome sights in the world. The Victoria Falls came close, but was still short. I could feel my eyes well with tears. We had done it! Driven 866km the last day, and 5625km in total. People had said we were crazy to try it. A woman and teenage daughter alone, I must be mental. Siobhan has only spent a year of her life in Cape Town, and although she loves the mountain, it doesn't quite mean as much to her as it does to me. She was more excited about the choice of music stations she found on the radio.

People I'd spoken to and information on the internet had said that Nairobi in Kenya to Cape Town was about 5000km. As Moshi is about 500km from Nairobi, I'd subtracted 500km from the total and come up with 4500km. The reality was very different. More than a 1000km different! That's an extra two days driving. Tired but beside ourselves with excitement, we turned into my brother David's road in Rondebosch at the foot of Table Mountain. We texted my son to let him know we were almost there. I couldn't help myself. Tears flowed freely as I stopped outside my brother's house and saw my son and my nephews standing on the sidewalk waving the South African flag. Maybe it's not just Table Mountain that does it for me.

Maybe, it's seeing my family and being part of them again after a time away.

> The Huguenot Tunnel on the **Du Toit's Kloof Pass** took 4 years to build and was opened in March 1988. The tunnel is 3.9km long, and the amazing thing is that when they were drilling and blasting to create the tunnel, when the two drilling heads that were coming from both sides met in the middle, they were only 3mm apart!

Stats for the day					
Odometer Start	**Odometer Finish**	**Day's Kilometres**	**Depart Time**	**Arrive Time**	**Hours travel**
181 060	181 926	866	06h00	16h30	10 and a half hours
Fuel	**Cost local currency**	**Cost US$**	**Accommodation**	**Cost local currency**	**Cost US$**
67.51 litres	R567.75	$73.83	Family	0	

Catching our breath

With the Football World Cup in full swing, Cape Town was a bustling hive of vibrant football supporters. People were blowing vuvuzelas in shopping malls as they watched the football games on large TVs. Everywhere you were faced with Football paraphernalia. Nobody living in Cape Town could escape the World Cup or forget it was on. The Victoria and Alfred Waterfront was humming, a sea of Orange on the day the Netherlands played. People who had never watched a football game in their lives caught the vibe and showed their support. It was amazing being there, a part of the vibe, and it made me proud to be a South African.

Jan van Riebeeck and other employees of the Dutch East India Company were sent to the **Cape of Good Hope** to establish a refreshment station to provide fresh food and water for passing ships travelling to and from the East. They landed in Table Bay on the 6 April 1652. Jan van Riebeeck and his men built a fort and laid out vegetable gardens and orchards. The Company Gardens are part of the original gardens and are situated at the top of Adderley Street in Government Avenue. Water from the Fresh River was used to provide irrigation. The Dutch settlers bartered with the native inhabitants for their sheep and cattle. Forests in Hout Bay and south and east of the mountain provided timber for ships and houses. At that time many animals were encountered in the Cape Peninsula. Some of these include the Cape Buffalo, elephant, hippopotamus, black rhinoceros, leopard, brown hyena, spotted hyaena, hunting dog, black-maned Cape Lion, black-backed jackal, silver fox, baboon, red hartebeest, eland, grysbok, klipspringer, duiker, bushbuck, aardvark, steenbok, rhebok, mongoose, genet, wildcat, hyrax and seal. Large birds found here were ostriches, secretary birds, black eagles and penguins. Nowadays you are only likely to meet up with a baboon or a hyrax when driving through a mountain pass.

The 68 000 seat **Cape Town Stadium** took 33 months to build at a cost of US$600 million. 2500 construction workers were employed to construct the stadium which boasts 500 toilets, 360 urinals, 115 entry turnstiles, 16 lifts in the building and a police station complete with jail. The site of the stadium is in the vicinity of where the **Green Point** Transit POW Camp was created to hold Boer prisoners-of-war during the Anglo-Boer War of 1899-1902. Altogether, 26 000 Boer prisoners were kept temporarily at the Green Point Camp before being transferred for internment in other parts of the British Empire. The British were afraid if they kept the prisoners in South Africa, they'd be freed by local sympathisers. Also, they had not anticipated the financial cost of the war and were struggling to feed their own troops and did not want the added burden of providing for POW's. So Boer POW's were sent to Bermuda, India, Ceylon and St. Helena.

In 1995, history was made when the imprint of a footprint was found embedded in rock on Cape Town's **West Coast**. Scientists dated it as being 117 000 years old – a great example of the existence of the earliest modern man. But then, it was identified as belonging to a woman... so it became known as "Eve's Footprint".

Relaxing, visiting family and friends, finding a flat for my son and getting him organised, shopping – sadly not much time for sight-seeing this visit. We'll have to come back for that. For those who've never visited Cape Town before, it is a glorious holiday destination. There is so much to do and see, ranging from getting quietly pissed on the Wine Route to diving with sharks, and the shopping malls are to die for. A must for everybody's bucket list of places to visit before you die.

Wolraad Woltemade is one of Cape Town's oldest heroes. He came to the Cape of Good Hope in the early 1700's as a dairyman for the Dutch East India Company. On 1st June 1773, a sailing ship, De Jonge Thomas, ran aground in Table Bay during a violent storm. As the ship broke up in the strong waves, the crowd watching on the beach were helpless and unable to save the lives of the survivors clinging to the hull. Wolraad rode his horse to the beach, to take food to his son who was a soldier on duty there. He couldn't bear to see the marooned sailors suffer, so he rode his horse into the sea. He made 7 trips, saving the lives of 14 people. On his last trip, 6 sailors tried to jump on his horse, the weight of them causing Wolraad and his horse to drown. Of the 151 people on the ship, 53 survived, 14 saved by Wolraad.

Our month in Cape Town was spent to-and-froing between my brother's house in Rondebosch and my parent's house in Hermanus. Hermanus is an hour's drive from Cape Town, and from August to October it is the best land-based whale-watching site in the world. The Southern Right Whales come into the bay to mate and calve. Hermanus also has the curious distinction of being the only town in South Africa to have a train station with no railway line. Someone jumped the gun there, anticipating a rail link that never came!

It's a sad fact of life that all good things have to come to an end, and our month-long holiday in Cape Town was no exception. It seemed like we had only just arrived, and then we had to leave. We'd spent the last week driving around with our car loaded up to the roof. Behind the two front seats was a wall of clothing and other goods we'd removed from storage and were taking back with us. That was probably tempting fate, and with our batteries charged and feeling refreshed, it was time to take to the road again. I have to confess, having enjoyed the down trip so much, I was looking forward to the up trip. We left not knowing exactly what route we'd be taking back. I just knew I wanted to take a different route. I just didn't know which road I'd be taking. I thought it would come to me along the way, like the 'Good Road Fairy' would put the idea in my head. What I did know, was that we'd be driving to Bloemfontein and staying with my aunt.

It's not just Table Mountain, all the mountains surrounding The Cape make it spectacular.

The first woman to climb **Table Mountain** was Lady Anne Barnard in 1790. She was quite a character and decided to climb the mountain only because no woman had ever done it before. She mounted a small expedition, which included three "gentlemen", several slaves and her personal maid. The group reached the summit via Platteklip Gorge and held a lavish picnic before descending.

Although the original plan to build a 'railway' to the top of table mountain was devised in 1870, the Anglo-Boer War and the First World war delayed matters, and it was only in 1926 that the plan was revived and the cableway completed in 1928. The cableway has since been upgraded four times, the last time being in 1997. Since 1929, over 20 million people have used the cableway to get to the top of Table Mountain. To this day, the Table Mountain Aerial Cableway has a proud history of being totally accident-free.

SOUTH AFRICA

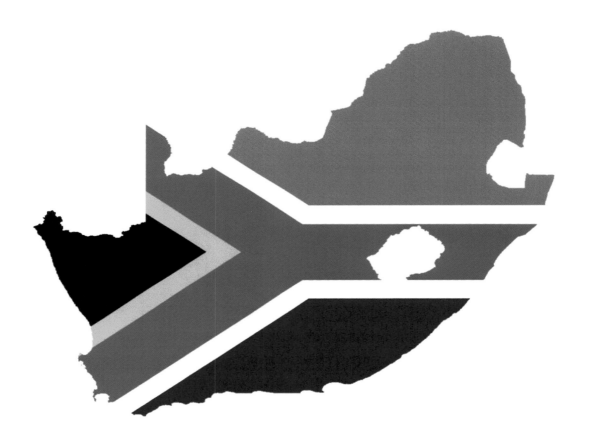

Car packed, fuel tank full, passports handy, ready to roll.

One of the great things about being a woman, is that you can change your mind at the last minute and that's okay. Initially, we'd decided to leave at 5am. The night before that changed to 5.30am and then 6am the latest. It was cold and dark when the alarm went off, so I decided to stay in the warm bed and snuggle under the covers until 6.15am and then get up. By the time I'd woken Siobhan up, put the last few items in the car and had a cup of coffee, it was 7.15am. Probably a far more reasonable hour to leave.

It was icy cold and I tried to cover my nose with the blanket that was wrapped all around me; even my hands on the steering wheel were under the blanket. I cursed myself for forgetting to find out how the car heater worked. I had remembered to have the car serviced which was just as well. The last person who had serviced it hadn't connected all the pipes back correctly and it was an actual miracle we'd made it down without mechanical problems. The mechanic also replaced the air filter which gave the car a heap more voomah! He said the air filter had a sand dune in it! I'd also managed to get the boot lock repaired so we were now able to open the boot door; not that you'd want to as a huge pile of who-knows-what would fall on you. Junk, we'd for whatever reason had decided was important enough to take back to Tanzania with us. As a fluffy purple poodle fell down from the pile stacked behind my headrest and landed on my lap dislodging my blanket, I had my doubts as to the reasoning behind some of our choices.

We went through the du Toit's Kloof Tunnel, the toll for which is R25, which is just under $4, and left Cape Town. Due to heavy cloud cover, there was no last minute sighting of Table Mountain as we drove up the mountain pass and entered the tunnel. There had been a light snowfall on the mountains again which caused a decidedly cool chill in the air. We stopped at Worcester's One Stop to buy plastic cups of hot chocolate and a toasted bacon and egg sandwich to have in the car. At Laingsburg an hour or so later we were still frozen and filled up with more hot chocolate. Siobhan discovered to her chagrin, that not only does hot chocolate stain, but it also burns when you spill it over yourself. Of course, this was my fault as everything that goes wrong always is, not that I know exactly what I did to make her spill half of her hot chocolate. While she stared out of the

window and sulked, I took pleasure in the peace of the desolate surroundings and the bleak landscape with the mountains looking like God had sprinkled icing sugar on them.

It seemed that not much progress had been made with the roadworks in the month since we'd last passed this way. I lost count of how many times from Laingsburg to Bloemfontein we had to sit and wait for 20 minutes while oncoming cars drove past, before we were allowed to resume our journey. We reached Beaufort West about five and a half hours after leaving Cape Town, and just picked up some hot pies for lunch which we could eat in the car. After this trip, no more junk food for me! One has a bit of a glut of it on long trips such as these. As this was going to be one of our longest driving stretches on our up trip, we didn't want to be delayed with sitting down to eat at Wimpy or some similar fast food restaurant.

Initially we'd planned Colesberg as a convenient bathroom stop along the way. However when we arrived the need wasn't there and we mistakenly decided to stop at another Ultra City or One Stop along the way to Bloemfontein. This was a bad decision, as there was no Ultra City or One Stop at any of the towns between Colesberg and Bloemfontein. There were fuel stops off the road which meant making a detour which wasn't what I wanted to do. I guess I was a bit mean and was probably still smarting over being blamed for her spilling her hot chocolate on herself, but every time we passed an off-road fuel stop and Siobhan was dozing, I continued driving. Unfortunately for her, she always seemed to wake up when we were in between towns and there were definitely no ablution facilities there! My advice, make a toilet stop in Colesberg even if you don't need it. There are no toilets between Colesberg and Bloemfontein.

Just after Colesberg I was stopped for speeding by the most inefficient traffic policeman on the force. He didn't note the fact that I had a foreign-registered car, and copied down my licence plate number incorrectly. I did tell him that I didn't live in South Africa, so he stupidly asked for my address when I used to live in South Africa. Of course, being a model citizen and having a very principled nature, I gave him the address of the house I lived in twenty years ago when I last lived in the country. Good luck to him finding me. I dispute that fine anyway, as I was driving slowly behind the car in front of me. He pulled both of us over, and he somehow had me travelling 15km an hour faster than the car I was trailing behind. Impossible. If that was accurate I would have smashed into the back of the car in front of me. When I queried it, he said that the handheld speed camera didn't lie. However, I have to ask with tears in my eyes, if he couldn't even read my licence plate number correctly, how the hell could he read the numbers on a speed camera? I neatly tore the speeding fine into small piece and disposed of it into my empty hot chocolate cup in the bag with all the other rubbish.

Colesberg is surrounded by little koppies which are small hills. The largest one, Coleskop, can be seen from a distance of 40km. The amazing thing about Coleskop, is no matter how much closer you travel towards it, it never seems to get any closer. Colesberg is the town where the first diamond found in Hopetown was identified as a diamond. Colesberg also played a part in the Anglo-Boer War. On the 14th November 1899, a 700-strong Boer Force took control of the town. On the 1st of January 1900, the British launched their attack. But it was only when the Boers retreated almost 2 months later that the British marched into the town unopposed on the 28th February 1900.

Crossing the Orange River on the Up Trip

We arrived in Bloemfontein at 7.15pm. It had taken us exactly 12 hours to get there, definitely one of our longest driving stints the whole trip. A delicious home-made lasagne and apple pie was waiting for us at my aunt's home. While we stayed at my aunt's house, there are many affordable accommodation choices in Bloemfontein. One of them being the Formule One Hotel which is reviewed elsewhere in this guide. The Formule Ones are scattered throughout major cities and traffic routes in South Africa, and all follow the same design and recipe. If you stay in one you know that the Formule One in the next town will look exactly the same. A bit like the McDonalds of the hotel industry. There are no unpleasant surprises with them, and they are relatively cheap in the big scheme of things.

Stats for the day					
Odometer Start	**Odometer Finish**	**Day's Kilometres**	**Depart Time**	**Arrive Time**	**Hours travel**
183828	184922	1094	07h15	19h15	12 hours
Fuel	**Cost local currency**	**Cost US$**	**Accommodation**	**Cost local currency**	**Cost US$**
86.85 litres	R697.60	$90.72	Family	0	0

Not having seen my aunt for close on thirty years, we had plenty to catch up on, so we weren't in a rush to get going. Our next stop was Pretoria which wasn't that far away. In Pretoria, I'd decided, I would finally decide on a route to take. My aunt made us a delicious bacon, egg and toast breakfast which went down well. We knew we had many take-away meals ahead of us.

As a child I'd seen the Vroue Monument (Women's Museum) from a distance and had always wanted to go there. While driving through Mafikeng and Kimberley, I'd told Siobhan a little about South African History and felt that a visit to the Vroue Monument would round it all off. Siobhan was a South African citizen after all, even though she'd only spent a year living in her home country. She should know something about the history. The Vroue Monument recognised the sacrifices of women and children of all races who were incarcerated in British Concentration Camps during the Anglo-Boer War. My aunt decided to go along with us and we all found the museum exhibits fascinating. Amazing what people can do to each other, the cruelty. One wonders if we can ever learn from the past as we seem to make the same mistakes over and over again.

Bloemfontein started out as a British fort in 1846, built on land purchased from the farmer Johannes Brits.

The writer, J. R. R. Tolkien, famous for *The Hobbit* and *Lord of the Rings*, was born in the city on 3 January 1892, though his family left South Africa following the death of his father.

From 1854 to 1898, Bloemfontein was the capital of the Orange Free State Republic, one of the Boer republics before the onset of the Anglo-Boer War. On 13 March 1900, following the Battle of Paardeberg, British forces captured the city and built a concentration camp nearby to house Boer women and children. The National Women's Memorial, on the outskirts of the city, pays homage to the 26,370 women and children as well as 1,421 old men and 15 000 farm workers who died in these camps.

We eventually left Bloemfontein just after midday, stopped to refuel and grab more take-aways for lunch, and go through the many tollgates along the road. I can never understand why you have to pay a toll to drive on a road people's income taxes are used to build. It's nonsense. Between Bloemfontein and Pretoria, you go through three different tollgates. At Verkeerderivier you are hit for R25; Grasmere R13; and Vaal R35. Now that might not seem like much, but when you add it up you come to R73 which is about $10!

When you cross the Vaal River, which is a tributary of the Orange River, then you know for sure that you are getting closer to Johannesburg. Traffic definitely seems to increase from this point and before you know it, you are stuck in bumper to bumper traffic on the N1 highway going through Johannesburg. Although Pretoria isn't that far from Johannesburg, the traffic jam you sit in to get there makes it feel miles further than it actually is. Now that Siobhan has decided that to read a map correctly, you have to do it upside down, we have more luck with her navigation skills. She'd managed to find the Formule One we were going to be staying in, on the map without a problem. "We have to find an exit saying Potgieter Street," she said looking out the window trying to read the exit signs on the turn-offs we were passing.

"Damn, what now!" I shouted as I suddenly found myself driving down a main road. "What the hell? There wasn't a sign, there wasn't a turn-off, how did we end up leaving the highway and ending up here?"

"Don't get mad at me, I never made you drive this way," Siobhan pointed out frantically studying the map again.

"The road just branched without any warning; now I don't know where the hell we are! Oh God, I don't believe it," I chuckled my annoyance evaporating as I read the street name on the sign post. "Potgieter Street. Luck must be on our side, the road branched off into Potgieter Street." It was quite easy to find the Formule One after that, although with all its one ways Pretoria is not my favourite town to drive in.

Soweto, the black township near Johannesburg and Pretoria, became famous during the Soweto Riots in the Apartheid Era on the 16 June 1976. Thousands of black students marched to the Orlando Stadium to protest having to learn Afrikaans at school. Some children started to throw stones, a police colonel panicked and fired a shot resulting in complete chaos. The government at the time said that only 23 people died. Other reports indicate between 200-600 people died during the riots. Nobody knows how many were injured, as doctors at hospitals were putting bullet wounds down as 'abscesses' in case the police targeted the families of the injured children.

Among the dead was Dr Melville Edelstein, who had devoted his life to social welfare among blacks.[9] He was stoned to death by the mob and left with a sign around his neck proclaiming 'Beware Afrikaaners'.

RECIPES FROM AFRICA - South Africa

Peri Peri Chicken Livers
This is a classic South African starter, served with toast fingers. Easy to make and very tasty. The secret is in the sauce. If you can't get your hands on brandy, then use sherry.
Ingredients
250g chicken livers
1 large onion cut into rings
2 tablespoons cooking oil
2 teaspoons peri peri spice, or cayenne pepper
Salt to taste
½ cup brandy
Method
1. Heat the oil in a frying pan and brown the onions.
2. Add the spices and mix together with the golden brown onions.
3. Add the chicken livers and mix together, making sure it doesn't stick to the bottom of the frying pan.
4. Add the brandy and let it simmer until the livers are cooked through.

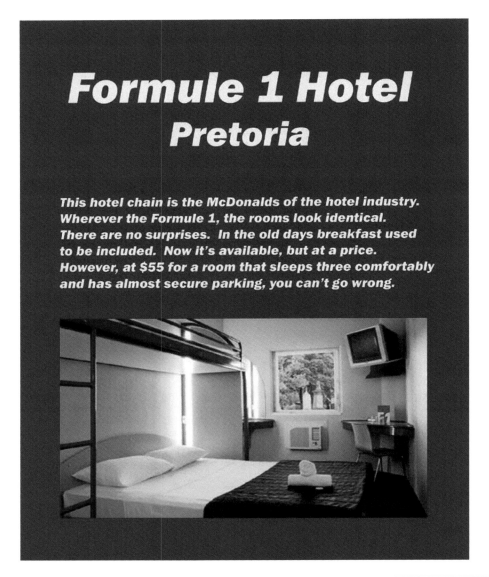

Formule 1 Hotel
Pretoria

This hotel chain is the McDonalds of the hotel industry. Wherever the Formule 1, the rooms look identical. There are no surprises. In the old days breakfast used to be included. Now it's available, but at a price. However, at $55 for a room that sleeps three comfortably and has almost secure parking, you can't go wrong.

Stats for the day					
Odometer Start	**Odometer Finish**	**Day's Kilometres**	**Depart Time**	**Arrive Time**	**Hours travel**
184922	185405	483	12h30	18h00	5 and a half hours
Fuel	**Cost local currency**	**Cost US$**	**Accommodation**	**Cost local currency**	**Cost US$**
74 litres	R614.95	$79.97	Formule 1 Hotel	R429	$55.79

Day Three: Pretoria to Louis Trichardt

I know I said this before, but I'm going to say it again. Pretoria is my least favourite South African city. And it isn't just the one way streets, it's the whole package. When we went down to the car the next morning, we saw that someone had tampered with both my spotlights. They'd hacksawed through the bolts holding the lights onto the bracket, but were either disturbed or didn't know how to detach them from the bottom bracket. The result was Missy doing a Santa's sleigh impersonation, the lights bouncing against the bracket making a jingling sound like the sleigh bells when we drove. And if that wasn't bad enough, with all the one way streets we struggled to find our way out of the city and back onto the highway. We did pass Paul Kruger's house. Three times.

During the Anglo-Boer War, when the British occupied Pretoria on 5 June 1900, Lord Alfred Milner established that gold to the value of approximately 2 million pounds had disappeared! This has led to the rumours of the **Kruger Millions** being buried somewhere in the Lowveld. There is documentation to show that a large quantity of gold was loaded onto a train on the 4th June 1900 and offloaded at Machadodorp where President Paul Kruger was residing at the time. Some say it was buried, others say it was sent to Mozambique and shipped to Europe. Kruger made his way to Mozambique and left on a ship to Holland on the 19th October 1900. There is no evidence he had any of the gold with him.

If I wasn't so frustrated with driving round in circles, we would have stopped off as part of our cultural history tour. Eventually, we found a road saying N1 which was the highway, although we weren't too sure which way to turn when we reached it. A sense of direction seems to be sadly lacking in our family. To make matters worse, town names had changed and I hadn't kept up to date with the new names, so had no idea where we should be travelling to. After reading the guide book the night before, I'd decided that we would chance our luck and drive through Zimbabwe. I wanted to drive through the Tete Corridor, which is a thin strip of land belonging to Mozambique which links Zimbabwe to Malawi. This would be the quickest route but a little risky. I made the mistake of mentioning to Siobhan that a few years ago, bandits used to hold up cars on the Tete Corridor. "If you drive that way, I'm walking back to Moshi," she snarled at me, obviously not having inherited my sense of adventure and love of dangerous circumstances. As I knew she didn't have any decent walking shoes with her, I succumbed to her wishes and said we'd detour through Zambia to get to Malawi.

I hadn't bothered about leaving at the crack of dawn as I knew we didn't have a big drive, so hung around the hotel to watch a Trinations Rugby game between the Springboks and the All

Blacks. I should have left at the crack of dawn. The gutted feeling and sadness at the Springbok's humiliating loss did nothing for my powers of concentration and observation skills. It was when the signs for Witbank became more and more frequent, that I realised we were on the wrong road and hopelessly lost. We'd left late at 12h15 and when the third person we asked for directions told us to drive the 100km back to Pretoria, I could feel my blood begin to boil and a stress migraine rise to the fore. After going through a tollgate, I pulled into a fuel station next to it and asked the manager to help us plot a route to Louis Trichardt on the big map they had on the wall. I remembered on previous occasions when I'd driven from Pretoria to Louis Trichardt, I'd gone through towns like Nylstroom and Potgietrsrus. When I looked at the big map, I realised to my horror that we were miles off track. We'd taken an enormous detour and would have to take back roads to get to Polokwane, which I knew as Pietersburg. One of the reasons I had gone so wrong as I never realised the road signs for Polokwane were pointing to the route I should be taking. So we took the scenic route through Groblersdal, where they sold the largest sweetest oranges, and Marble Hall before coming out at Polokwane. Then it was easy to follow the road to Louis Trichardt.

Polokwane World Cup Stadium

To get to Louis Trichardt, you have to go through yet another Toll Plaza. The Capricorn Toll Plaza, obviously named after its proximity to the Tropic of Capricorn. This time it cost R29, which is roughly $4. The exhaust I had fixed in Cape Town started sounding suspect again, maybe because of a couple of the gravel roads I had had to drive on and some of the bad potholes we disappeared into. That was not a good sign, and other than buying some oranges, it was not proving to be a good day. Siobhan had been feeling increasingly car sick because of the winding roads. Like most people, she is not pleasant company when she feels sick.

Louis Trichardt has grown considerably since I lived there twenty years ago. It has a large shopping mall, and in the dark I had no idea which direction to drive to find the main road. I knew that twenty years ago there was a Spur Steak Ranch on the main road. I was hoping that it would still be there, and that the prospect of barbecued ribs would make Siobhan feel better. Amazingly enough, we lucked on the main road and the Spur was still there. We were like prisoners ready to put in our order for our last meal. The silly child made the mistake of ordering a second milkshake when she'd finished the first. I did tell her that too much dairy wasn't good for nausea, but who am

I and what do I know? Half-way through her second milkshake, she felt too nauseous to finish her meal. The waitress was brilliant, sympathised with Siobhan which made her feel better, and gave us detailed instructions how to find a guesthouse to spend the night in. With doggy bag full of ribs in tow, we drove around town trying to follow the waitress's directions. Unfortunately, in the dark we weren't sure what constituted a four-way stop or not and got lost. We found another hotel, but it was rather pricey and had a very noisy bar filled with very drunk people singing at the top of their voices. They must have been All Black supporters still celebrating the morning's victory. I thought I'd given finding the Zebra Inn Backpackers one last go, and in trying to find our way back to the main road, accidentally stumbled upon the Zebra Inn. We seemed to be getting rather good at finding places by accident.

The Zebra Inn Backpackers was dirt cheap. Accommodation was in a shed built in the garden with curtain cubicles for bedrooms, rather like a hospital ward. One of the cubicles was already occupied when we got there. The owner of the Backpackers assured us that the parking was safe in his yard as he locked the gate. He said that he'd had no burglaries all the years he'd lived there. Later on, when he was showing us the TV Lounge set up under an open thatched lapa next to the dormitory, he explained that if we watched TV we had to take the TV set and lock it up in the dorm with us when we went to bed. Two weeks before, he'd had a burglary and the robbers had stolen the DVD player and television from the TV Lounge. I don't think he even realised that he'd contradicted what he'd told us earlier.

The man in the cubicle at the end of the room had a really bad cough and wheezed when he walked to spit his phlegm into who knows where. The sound of his retching was so loud, it seemed to echo through the shed dormitory. It was quite creepy and a little disgusting listening to him. Siobhan was terrified and kept begging me to rather find another place for the night. However, with three duvets covering me I was warm and snug and not keen to leave that warmth to find another guesthouse or hotel in the middle of the night. I instructed Siobhan to try and be brave, and luckily she soon fell asleep.

The town of **Louis Trichardt** was named after a Voortrekker who arrived there in 1836 after trekking north. Trichardt and his group stayed near the Soutpansberg Mountains, camping near what eventually became the town . They planted crops and started exploring the area northwards in an attempt to locate another Voortrekker and his group. After spending a year in the area, they decided to head for Lourenço Marques, a journey that took them 7 months to complete, during which more than half the group perished including Trichardt himself.

In 2003, the name of the town was changed from Louis Trichardt to Makhado, after a Venda king who ruled the area from 1864 until 1895. In September 2005, a statue of the Venda King was unveiled, while a statue of Louis Trichardt was removed and stored in a tool shed. The statue of Makhado was painted the colours of the old South African flag only six days later, apparently by those opposing the name change. The statue of Louis Trichardt was later moved to a public library. The controversy in this small town continued when a group consisting of Shangaan, Pedi and Indian residents, who felt that the Venda king Makhado had been a nasty oppressor, appealed the name change. On the 29th March 2007, the Supreme Court Appeal (SCA) ruled in favour of an appeal to reverse the name change ordered in June 2003. Makhado was changed back to Louis Trichardt. Currently, the SA Geographical Names Council are hearing presentations to change the name back to Makhado again.

Zebra Inn Backpackers
Louis Trichardt

Very basic, no privacy and and the mystery guest sharing the dorm was a little creepy. But at $23 a night for two people, you couldn't expect much more at that price. You get what you pay for. We weren't brave enough to use the shower as the lock on the door didn't work. The beds were comfortable and warm.

Stats for the day					
Odometer Start	**Odometer Finish**	**Day's Kilometres**	**Depart Time**	**Arrive Time**	**Hours travel**
185405	185881	476	12h15	18h30	6 and a quarter hours
Fuel	**Cost local currency**	**Cost US$**	**Accommodation**	**Cost local currency**	**Cost US$**
64.66 litres	R525.04	$68.28	Zebra Inn Backpackers	R180	$23.41

Zimbabwe

As I was a little nervous about the Zimbabwe border, having only heard negative comments, I didn't sleep too well. Despite her anxiety the night before, Siobhan slept like the dead, so I left her sleeping and went to see if I could score a cup of coffee in the kitchen of the main house. While chatting to the owner of the backpackers, another guest walked into the kitchen. I nearly dropped my coffee cup when he said, "Oh my God, Cindy?" He was my ex-husband's old boss when we lived in Louis Trichardt 20 years ago! When you travel a lot, it seriously is a very small world, and you often bump into people you've met in the past in the strangest of places. Like the Zebra Inn Backpackers in Louis Trichardt. After a quick catch-up, Siobhan woke up and stumbled into the kitchen looking for me. We had a quick wash, brushed the teeth and decided to head down to the Mall to have breakfast and try and find some car-sickness pills for Siobhan. We'd left buying a vuvuzela until the last minute, which was a bit silly as everywhere you went they were sold out. The Mall was no exception. We did find car-sickness pills for Siobhan, which she took with her breakfast. We left Louis Trichardt with the Soutpansberg Mountains making a beautiful backdrop, and took the road to Messina.

View of Louis Trichardt from the Soutpansberg Mountains

The Soutpansberg Tunnels are a delight for motorbike enthusiasts who love speeding through bends and winding roads, but for someone with car sickness it could be hair-raising. My panic was not the winding tunnels, but the fact that my car lights didn't appear to be working properly. No lights came on whatsoever on my dashboard, so I couldn't check my speedometer, and the beams from the headlights were so weak, they were negligible. I try to avoid driving at night, but still it does happen and having no lights would put us in a pretty bad situation! It was only when we exited from the tunnels, that I realised I had my sunglasses on, hence it still appearing to be dark with the lights on. However, the fuse on the dashboard must have gone, because the dashboard light never worked for the remainder of the trip.

Messina has the most amazing baobab trees. I think besides being a border town, that's the only other thing going for it. The town itself is small and dusty. I wanted to find the police station to get some copies of my passport certified. In South Africa the police can certify documents for you at police stations for no charge. In Tanzania, only lawyers who are notary publics can certify documents, and they charge for the privilege. Despite signs on the road indicating there was a police station, it wasn't easy to find and we eventually ended up at the Messina jail at lunch time, without realising we were at the jail. There were no signs saying 'JAIL', just plenty of police vehicles around. We walked through the big gates which were open, joining the crowd of women walking in, and followed them to a table manned by two policewomen. Across from the table, was a large zinc iron shed without any windows, but with a large bolted gate blocking any escape for the men locked up inside. This it appeared, was the Messina jail. The women were bringing the men their lunch. Obviously, no meals are provided in this establishment. The prisoners were all pushing against the gate, trying to make contact with their women on the other side. Siobhan was scared, thinking all the prisoners were going to escape and attack us. With all the armed policemen around, this was highly unlikely, and she wasn't very impressed when I ignored her fear and told her if she was that scared she could sit in the car. A policewoman signed and certified my documents, and we were ready to drive to the Zimbabwe border.

Of course, they make sure that you get hit for one last road toll before you leave South Africa. The Baobab Toll Plaza charges you R28 or $4. We refuelled at the Ultra City on the South African side of the border, not too sure what the fuel situation would be like in Zimbabwe. We had heard differing rumours. Some said there were still chronic fuel shortages. Others that there was no longer any problem getting fuel. As the jerry can was covered in stuff, we decided to take our chances and find fuel in Zimbabwe.

The South African border post was busy being renovated and there were tents set up where different officials worked. My hearts went out to them, as the tents were stuffy and hot. Imagine maintaining a good mood in those conditions! When we asked for directions to Immigration, they said, "Go to the tent." There were no signs pointing to the tent. In fact, there were three tents so it was hard to find the right one. The second tent we tried proved to be Immigration and I asked the woman working there if we could borrow her pen as I'd left mine in the car. "Go to Duty Free and buy one," was her acid response. Obviously the heat and lack of fresh air did affect their demeanour. My concern about getting across the border without having proper entry papers into South Africa was all for nought. Now that we were leaving, they didn't care that the border post in Zeerust didn't follow the proper process and that we had no temporary import papers. With no papers to stamp, they took our Botswana import papers and waved us through. Although there were quite a few trucks lined up at the border, they didn't affect us. All those warnings about how long you take at the Beit bridge border post were for nothing. Mind you, it could be because we were crossing at lunch time on a Sunday.

The horror stories of the Zimbabwe border post at Beit Bridge proved to be unfounded. Well, for us at any rate. There weren't any queues, just plenty of people you had to see for the necessary stamp on a piece of paper. We sailed through immigration, paid the R80 cross border fee for the driver and the R250 road toll and carbon tax, and waved away the two or three 'agents' who tried to foist their services on us. "You need us!" the one shouted as we entered the police clearance building, "Look at your car! It's so over-loaded they are going to want you to unpack and charge you tax! Don't be a fool and take a chance. You want us to help you." No sonny, actually we didn't. We were doing quite fine by ourselves. The CID at police clearance were a bit confused about the Tanzanian system, where the Tanzanian Road Authority takes your original car registration card when you leave the country and give you a certified copy of the original to take with you on your travels. But they seemed to understand when I explained it to them for the fifth time. They stamped our certified copy and told us to proceed to the customs supervisor.

After what those agents had said, I decided that the friendly cheerful approach was necessary. The customs supervisor was a young woman not much over twenty. We struck up a conversation, chatting about her job and her life and then I mentioned that we were relocating to Tanzania and our car was very full. "Drive it around and I'll take a look," she said with what I hoped was a friendly smile. Not a shark's smile before it bit your leg off. We duly drove the car to her and she looked through the windows. "Hmm," she said, "Obviously relocating. You may go through,' and she passed us an exit pass to give to the guard at the gate. I couldn't hide my smile of satisfaction, as I waved goodbye to the agents who were staring at us with their mouths open, absolutely stunned that we got through so easily. The whole border crossing at both sides of the border had taken us a total of one and a half hours. Nothing at all like we'd been told, so I guess it was one of our lucky days.

On the Zimbabwe side there was a big fuel station with a Wimpy attached. Knowing that Wimpy's quality is pretty standard, we decided to go there for lunch before continuing on to Masvingo. They had the Wimpy posters up, the Wimpy menus on the wall and the special Wimpy ketchup and mustard bottles on the tables. The waitresses even wore special Wimpy uniforms. That's where the similarity to Wimpy ended. When the waitress didn't bring me a menu, I assumed it was because they didn't have the items on the menu. "What do you have?" I asked looking at the pictures of burgers on the walls.

"We have fish and chips or T-bone steak and chips. That's all"

"I'm still feeling sick, I'll just have a coke," Siobhan said slouching over the table, her face a greenish shade of white.

"Sorry. No coke."

"Then I'll have a fanta," Siobhan was sticking to brand names she knew.

"Sorry. No fanta. Only local soft drinks."

This was the most un-Wimpyish Wimpy I'd ever been to. I wondered if the Wimpy Head Office knew about it. But, if they didn't, I wasn't going to report them. There was just something so sad about a Wimpy having no coke and no burgers. It made a statement about the state of the country, and the professionalism of the workforce who still went about their work, even though they no longer had the products to sell. Siobhan and I shared a T-bone steak and chips and I left a hefty tip. It was the least I could do and I have to say, that T-bone was so tender, one of the best I've ever had!

The road to Masvingo took us through bush, past over-run farms and ruined labourer's cottages; all that is left of a once proud agricultural nation. We also passed through two road blocks which doubled up as road tolls. The toll is US$1, or R10. They have their own exchange rate. Zimbabwe had scrapped the Zim dollar and is now using both US dollars and South African rand. The exchange rate differs from person to person, place to place. You definitely get more for US$ though. They rip you off quite a bit with their South African Rand exchange rate.

At 5.30pm we arrived in Masvingo, and checked into the first hotel we saw which was the Chevron, which must have been very grand many years ago. In retrospect, we should have driven around and looked at some others; for what you get the Chevron is very over-priced. It is handily located, and does have secure parking. They make a note of your car's contents and how much fuel your gauge shows, just in case someone hops over the wall at night and empties your car of fuel and contents. The guard's eyes did go wide as he saw the contents of our car. "Too much to write," he said incredulously, as he just wrote down 'HOUSEHOLD GOODS AND CLOTHING.'

For the $90 they did give us a family room, which consisted of a main bedroom with a huge bed and TV and another room with twin beds. Of course, Siobhan being Siobhan, she immediately plonked herself down on the double bed and turned on the TV. Room service brought us plates of steaming hot beef stew and sadza, the traditional maize meal porridge with the same consistency as mashed potato. Delicious.

RECIPES FROM AFRICA - Zimbabwe

Pumpkin in Peanut Sauce
Very yummy and easy to make. Great as a side dish. Serves 4.
Ingredients
½ cup water
½ pumpkin peeled and cut into small cubes
4 tablespoons peanut butter
Salt to taste
Method
 First boil the water in a pot then add the pumpkin cubes. When pumpkin is soft and you can easily test its softness with a fork, add the peanut butter. Stir the pot contents together. Pour out excess water and mash.

Chevron Hotel Masvingo

This hotel is a little dated and very over-priced for what you get. We were impressed with the professionalism of the staff in what must be tough working conditions. There are almost daily power cuts. If there were 4 of us, then the $90 a night would not be too expensive

We were given a family room which consisted of two bedrooms and a shared bathroom. Breakfast was included.

Stats for the day					
Odometer Start	**Odometer Finish**	**Day's Kilometres**	**Depart Time**	**Arrive Time**	**Hours travel**
185881	186298	417	10h15	17h30	7 and a quarter hours
Fuel	**Cost local currency**	**Cost US$**	**Accommodation**	**Cost local currency**	**Cost US$**
65.43 litres	R553	$71.91	Chevron Hotel	$90	$90

During the excavations at **Great Zimbabwe** by European archaeologists, eight stone carvings of soapstone birds were unearthed. Their distinctive curved shape was thought to represent the bateleur eagle. One of the **stone birds** was sent to Cecil Rhodes in Cape Town. This remains in the Groote Schuur Estate in Cape Town, Rhodes's former home. This is the only bird not currently in Zimbabwe. Rhodes became fixated with the stone bird and managed to procure an additional four complete birds and a partial bird. These were returned on independence. Pieces of another stone bird were discovered in a museum in Germany and reunited with the remaining piece in Zimbabwe. The eighth and final statue has always remained in Zimbabwe.

Our wake-up coffee and tea they'd offered us the night before never arrived. We hung around our room watching a movie on TV waiting in case they had just got their times wrong, but the wake-up hot drinks never arrived. One has the feeling the staff go through the motions, doing what they've been trained to do, but not having enough tea and coffee to actually do the wake-up calls. This feeling was reinforced when we finally went down to the dining room for breakfast. The breakfast buffet appeared a decent spread, and you could order sausage, eggs and bacon which was served on chipped plates that had seen better days. There were even freshly baked scones. However, the waiter apologised profusely when we asked if he had jam or marmalade. "I am so terribly sorry," he said in a colonial British accent, "But we've been out of jam and marmalade for a while."

At 9.15am we collected our car from the secure parking area, and left to see the Great Zimbabwe Ruins. These are the ruins that gave Zimbabwe its name. We missed the road to the ruins and ended up at a beautiful lake. Although there were resorts, camping sites and chalets advertised there on old weather-damaged sign posts, given what we'd experienced thus far in Zimbabwe, I'm not sure how good the quality of the accommodation would be. There was one that sounded nice from its advertising board – Kyle View Chalets. However, we didn't go and check it out.

Lake Kyle or Lake Mutirikwi as it is now known as

The entrance fee to the ruins is $15 an adult and $8 a child. We signed the visitor's book and noticed that we were the first visitors to the ruins in ten days. How sad is that? A World Heritage Site, it should be a major tourist destination, but it was completely devoid of tourists. All the staff are there, manning their positions, the tour guides dressed up smartly, waiting day in and day out for some tourists to arrive. How soul-destroying for them, heart-wrenching for me. What a waste of a beautiful country, friendly people just waiting to share their expertise with others. I couldn't do that. Get dressed and go to work on the off-chance that some people might just show. I can remember the last time I'd travelled to Zimbabwe and the ruins, fourteen years ago. The road to the ruins was lined with local craftsmen selling their soapstone statues, baskets, batiks and other hand-painted fabrics. Now the roads were empty, only a couple of craftsmen selling their wares. It was very depressing.

The Zimbabwe Ruins were smaller than I'd remembered but still a sight to behold. There has been so much speculation as to who built the ruins. It's gone from King Solomon to Arab

Traders, and now they say it's the Shona people who built them. I'm not convinced. What I did find interesting, was the hundreds-year-old Chinese porcelain that had been found at the site. It makes me think that Zheng He, the famous Chinese explorer from the early fourteen hundreds, had reached there. There were so many monkeys around the ruins, it would have been great if I could perform magic and turn them all into tourists. Unfortunately, although I've been many things in my life, a magician is not one of them.

We were thrilled to see another couple arrive just as we were exploring the last piles of ruins in the valley. At least the staff would have something to do! The guy watching the museum and acting as a guide for those who needed one proved to be very knowledgeable. He showed us the old stone birds that have been returned to Great Zimbabwe. They are displayed under heavy security, with state of the art security cameras following your every move while you view them in a special secure room. Unfortunately, you are not allowed to take photos of anything inside the museum, especially the stone birds. We heard drums beating and singing. People in the village in the valley were celebrating something, the village women were dancing. We wondered if it was for our

benefit. As if, they were told there were tourists and they were putting on a performance for us, hoping we'd pay them something. As we were in a hurry to get going to Harare, we didn't go to the village to watch, but did notice the other tourist couple making their way to the village with their camera and its extra-long lens.

From Masvingo to Harare we went through two $1 toll stops, two big police road blocks with soldiers carrying guns and passed twelve traffic police holding speed cameras. We didn't manage to pass through all of that unscathed though. Right outside Masvingo I was stopped for travelling 71km in an 80km zone. The police were hiding behind a big tree, and stopping motorists as they increased speed from the 60km zone to the 80km area. How unfair was that? To call the policewomen belligerent would be an understatement. They were both ready for a fight. The man who stopped us seemed docile in comparison and stood in the background with an embarrassed smile on his face. He knew they were in the wrong, as I measured it; they were 30m into the 80km zone when they were stopping motorists. The Zimbabweans they'd stopped were furious and there was a lot of shouting going on. I was definitely wearing my boxing gloves which was probably not a good thing as it nearly landed me in jail.

"We are stopping speeding motorists to keep the road safe," the one policewoman shouted above the angry motorists' voices.

"If you wanted to keep the roads safe, you wouldn't hide behind a tree and jump out and nearly cause the motorists to have an accident!" I shouted back to the delight of the gathering crowd.

"Yes! Yes! She's right!" The men from the crowd shouted back and I sensed that I was inciting a riot.

Fuelled by their support, I continued. "If you wanted to make the road safe you'd make yourselves visible so motorists slow down. When you hide away you have no intention of making them drive slower, you want them to go fast so you can fine them!"

I should have stopped when the policewoman writing out the fines broke her pen in half. Some of my supporters stepped back. Oblivious to the impending danger, I continued, "You are stopping us in the 80km zone, that's a criminal offence. You are the ones breaking the law." Of course I had no idea if it was a criminal offence, but it sounded good.

"Don't pay the fine then! Object, I'd love that. Let's go now. You can sit in jail while we wait for the case to come up and then you tell the judge how you are not guilty and shouldn't pay the fine." The woman snarled and her face twisted. She really was one of the ugliest women I'd ever seen, especially the way her mouth was distorted in her rage. Siobhan was still in the car and just heard the word 'jail.' Of course, she panicked.

"Mom! Calm down, just pay the fine! Mom! Stop!"

I hate being cheated out of money. And to make matters worse, even though the exchange rate was R7.50 to the US$, the Zimbabwean Traffic Police were charging R10 to the US$. So, my $20 cost me R200! I was furious, but had no desire to be arrested. When I tried to give them the fine money, they refused to take it. "You say we are thieves, let's rather go to court, come on, you can give us a lift to town."

I pointed to my tightly packed car and asked sweetly if they'd like to sit on the roof or on the bonnet. They didn't reply, but the woman who broke the pen snatched the money out of my hand while the other wrote out the fine. As I walked back to my car carrying the speeding fine I crumpled it into a ball and threw it over my shoulder. I'm sure they were watching, but I never turned around to look.

There were plenty of fuel stations between Masvingo and Harare. Unfortunately, none of them had fuel. Once again, like other workers we'd seen, the pump attendants were all at work, ready to meet and greet motorists with thirsty vehicles. Their job was to tell them, "Sorry no fuel. Try again in a few days." Of course this was not very helpful when the fuel tank is empty.

Apart from the police officers hiding behind bushes holding speed cameras, we saw plenty of vervet monkeys along the road. What we were anxiously searching for, was a road sign telling us

how far away we were from Harare. The fuel light had come on and we were having nail-biting moments. I cursed myself for burying the jerry can under 'stuff.' Actually, the 'stuff' had seemed a good idea at the time. As our car was so full, dragging a suitcase out of the car each time we stopped for the night and finding a hole to push it back into just seemed a potential nightmare. So, I'd come up with this cunning plan to work out how many days we'd be travelling, and pack each day's clothes for both Siobhan and I into plastic supermarket carry bags. When we removed the clean clothes from a bag, we'd fill it with the dirty clothes we'd just taken off and tie up the bag so that we knew the clothes were used, worn and dirty. An untied bag meant clean clothes. So far the plan had worked well, but it did mean that the bags completely covered the jerry can which was somewhere underneath them. When the sign indicating we were 40km from Harare appeared, we both started to cheer. I knew then that we should just make it into Harare.

Siobhan had been studying the travel guide and picked out a backpackers she thought we could try for the night. It did sound great, with the dorms in tree houses and a great vibe. Well, that's what the guide book said. Now I have to tell you this. Don't bother with a guide book in Zimbabwe. Most of the accommodation choices mentioned in the guides no longer exist. They all went out of business when the tourist industry completely collapsed during Zimbabwe's troubled years. Once again, we accidentally found ourselves on the right road, in this case, Robert Mugabe Drive. It wasn't anything we did, or Siobhan's superior navigating skills. I asked her what road we needed to be on; she replied Robert Mugabe and we both looked up and that was the road we were on. We were on the lookout for Hillside Backpackers. We turned right off Robert Mugabe into Chirembe, then immediately left into Hillside which isn't very well sign-posted. I have to say, most of the traffic lights in Harare didn't work, which made driving through them an exciting and somewhat dangerous adventure. We looked at the guide book and confirmed the address, 71 Hillside. We looked at 71 Hillside and could just make out the remains of some tree houses in the trees. Hillside Backpackers were no more. The main house, once quite stately, was a dilapidated wreck. Luckily, there were people living there and they told us of another place in the area which took in backpackers. It was literally round the corner. On Hillside from the sorry tree houses, you take the first right and then the first right again. You continue driving until you get to 20 le Roux Road.

There were no signs indicating it was a backpackers, a few cars parked on the lawn, some men sitting outside having a BBQ. It was starting to get dark and I didn't relish the idea of driving around Harare at night to try and find accommodation. The men came to our car which must have looked a sight packed to the roof. "Can we help you?"

"Is this Hillside Backpackers?" I asked hesitantly, thinking I must have gone to the wrong house.

The man stroked his grey beard. "We do sometimes take in backpackers, but we're full now. I don't think we have room." He looked at all our 'stuff' in the car. "Where have you come from?"

"Cape Town," Siobhan added quickly. "We're on our way to Tanzania."

The man pulled on his beard thoughtfully. "We'd better make a plan for you then. $10 a night each, but if it's too expensive I can make it cheaper." I nearly jumped out the car and kissed him. $20 in total a night was a miracle for us! "Go down the road to the Spar, get yourself some meat and you can throw it on the fire. I'll go and make space for the both of you." He was maybe not the chattiest, but his heart was definitely in the right place!

The Spar Supermarket was extremely well-stocked. You can buy anything in Harare! They had shelves laden with jams and marmalades, so I guess the Chevron Hotel in Masvingo should

travel up to Harare to do their shopping! We bought steak and sausage and some bread rolls. We returned to the house to find that the owner, Ian, had cleared his room for us. We sat chatting around the fire, Ian and the other guys telling us Zim stories, things that happened during the tough time the country went through. I went to bed that night knowing that I was blessed and never had to endure some of the things the Zimbabweans endured.

RECIPES FROM AFRICA – **Zimbabwe**

Sadza

Maize meal porridge is a staple in many African countries. It looks and tastes the same but goes by different names. Sadza in Zimbabwe, Ugali in Tanzania, Nshima in Zambia and Malawi, Pap or Putu in South Africa. The stiffness of the porridge depends on how much water you add. For a softer porridge suitable for breakfast, use double the amount of water. One thing you have to make sure of though, is that the cooking heat is just right. Too hot and the porridge will burn, so stir continuously. Ingredients for 6-8 people
5 litres water
Salt to taste
2 cups maize meal
Method
 Boil the water and add the salt. The next step can be done in two different ways. Either gradually add the maize meal stirring all the time until it is well mixed with the water. Or, mix the two cups of maize meal with some of the water to make a thin paste and then add that to the boiling water. Cover and cook over a low heat until cooked through. Give it a stir every now and then to prevent it from sticking to and burning on the bottom. You know it's done when it starts to pull away from the sides and forms a ball in the middle of the pot.

Hippo Pools
Harare

Ian owns a bush camp and the house on Le Roux Road is just his office. But he took us in anyway, gave us his bed and charged us $20 for the night!

Stats for the day					
Odometer Start	Odometer Finish	Day's Kilometres	Depart Time	Arrive Time	Hours travel
186298	186702	404	12h15	16h30	4 and a quarter hours
Fuel	Cost local currency	Cost US$	Accommodation	Cost local currency	Cost US$
8.8 litres	$10	$10	Hippo Pools backpackers	$20	$20

Day Six: Harare to Chirundu

After an uncomfortable night's sleep with the lumpiest pillow I'd ever encountered in my life, I still managed to wake up feeling refreshed and ready for whatever the day held. My first mission for the day was to check my bank balance on the internet, and then find a working ATM so that I could draw some money to refuel the car. As easy as that task may sound – no more than an irksome errand, it would seem - in Harare, capital city of Zimbabwe, it could prove to be quite an arduous task. The night before, the men staying with Iain had regaled me with tales about the Zimbabwean dollar just before it was phased out. How the one guy, Keith, had put a bag full of money in his safe, gone down to South Africa for three weeks, and when he came back, the money he had put away to last for a month was only enough to buy a loaf of bread! That craziness, although over with replacing the Zim $ with the US$, had still left its mark. The ATM machines were unreliable at best, and nobody knew of any which took foreign ATM cards. This could be a huge set-back for us. Without money, we would not be able to leave Zimbabwe. Iain offered to loan us some US$, but I was determined to find the one ATM in Harare which must surely take foreign visa cards.

While we were waiting for the power to come back on so we could fire up the internet and computer, Keith made me a cup of coffee and told me some more Zimbabwe stories. The one that really moved me, was the story of a farmer friend of his who had his farm invaded by 'war veterans'. The farmer had to leave everything behind and flee with his family. One of his workers was an ex- Selous Scout tracker. Three years after the invasion, this worker contacted some of the farmer's friends and said that he needed to meet urgently with him. There was unfinished business that needed to be sorted out. The farmer was a bit nervous about meeting his old worker, fearing it could be some kind of a set up and if he met him his life might be in danger. But being the curious sort, agreed to a meeting. Imagine his surprise when the worker met him with bags of money. For three years he had been stealing the farmer's farm implements from the war veterans who had taken over the farm, and selling them. He'd kept all the money for three years until he'd sold all the implements, so that the farmer could get some of his investment back!

103

The big tragedy for me, is the death of the Tourism Industry in Zimbabwe. Obviously this has had adverse effects on the economy and people's livelihoods. Iain Jarvis owns this amazing bush camp called Hippo Pools Wilderness Camp. This rustic camp plays an important role in eco-tourism for the area and in the awareness of the Umfurudzi Safari Area. Aparently, it's stunningly located in a secluded spot on the Mazowe River and takes its name from the large pool it overlooks and which is usually occupied by hippo. There are chalets, cabins and campsites. Meals can be provided if you wish. But besides the abundant bird life, the amazing thing is that there are over 250km of mapped paths and hiking trails within the camp's operational area, ranging from easy, marked trails along the Mazowe River to more challenging ones. You can go bird viewing, hiking, game viewing, tiger fishing, kayaking, swimming in an untouched wilderness area! How cool is that? If we weren't in a hurry to get on with the rest of our trip, I'd loved to have made a detour and gone to stay at Hippo Pools Wilderness camp. Because of the lack of tourists, you can get to stay at these amazing places for bargain rates. Iain charges $10 per person per night for a chalet, $5 per person per night for a cabin, and $2 a person for night for the campsite. Iain Jarvis can be contacted on +263 0913 043 828 or 0912 337 355 wildernessafrica@zol.co.zw. Hippo Pools is only about 150km from Harare.

As we were leaving Iain Jarvis's house in Harare to go on a search for a working ATM, the doctor staying with Iain came running out to our car. "My brother has a camp as well! I heard you talking to Iain, can you please put my brother's info in your book? He's desperate for guests to keep it going!" Okay doctor, here it is. Steve Edwards steve.musango@microlink.zim +263 712207307 www.musanngosafaricamp.com. Steve owns the Musango Safari Camp which is on an island in Lake Kariba. If you drive to Kariba, they'll pick you up. They have black rhino, birding, the big five and absolutely incredible fishing – tiger fish and bream. If you think of some of the prices you have to pay in other African countries to go on safari, Zimbabwe is definitely worth considering as a holiday destination. Just take some spare fuel and bring a stash of US$ so that you don't have to rely on ATMs!

We drove around for a good hour trying different ATM machines, but no luck. After receiving many different directions, we finally found Sam Levy Village, which was a shopping mall which looked as if it had been lifted from South Africa and transplanted into Harare. We tried the Barclays ATM and it worked! It appeared to be the only ATM in all of Zimbabwe which not only takes foreign cards, but can also dispense cash! To celebrate we decided to go to one of the very nice looking cafés at the mall for breakfast. Unfortunately, they could not make waffles as their machine was broken, but we were able to order delicious croissants. We managed to get directions on how to leave Harare and find the road to Kariba. It was far simpler than I had imagined. Of course, getting fuel was another small problem, but luckily we only had to wait 30 minutes at the fuel station for them to take a fuel delivery first, and then we were able to fill our tank.

We ended up leaving Harare at 11.30am, stopped off at Chinhoyi to use the toilet at the Caltex garage there and managed to proceed without incident. We did count eight speed cameras on the way to the border, and went through two tolls. The first toll did try a fast one, saying they had no change, but I persisted and didn't move forward, just sat there with my hand out the window waiting for my change while cars behind me started hooting in impatience, and eventually they gave me my money and we continued with our journey. The trip to the border was uneventful. We did see tantalizingly fresh piles of elephant dung on the road, but no elephants.

Operation Noah was a wildlife rescue operation in the then Rhodesia, now called Zimbabwe, lasting from 1958 to 1964. Lake Kariba was created on the Zambezi River when the world's largest man-made dam - a hydroelectric power station was built across the Zambezi River, about 400km from Victoria Falls. In the process it flooded the Zambezi Valley, home to thousands of wild animals. In a wildlife rescue operation led by Rupert Fothergill, over 6000 animals (elephant, antelope, rhino, lion, leopard, zebra, warthog, small birds and even snakes) were rescued and relocated to the mainland.

Chirundu, the small town on the border between Zimbabwe and Zambia, is so small that you blink your eyes and you miss it. Just before the town, we did spot a green Landrover with three European-looking men sitting on the back holding rifles. They appeared to be hunters. I hope they weren't poachers but my guess is that poachers wouldn't be quite so brazen.

To get to the bridge, you have to wend your way through lines of trucks double-parked along the narrow road. It all appears quite chaotic, but once on the bridge and at the actual border, it is far more organised and no traffic at all. The border post has Zimbabwe and Zambia sharing the same building.

To be honest, what later transpired was completely unexpected. The day had gone quite well. We'd managed to find an ATM that worked, filled our car with petrol, avoided being caught by speed cameras. It had been a good, uneventful day. We did our customary smile and chat at the immigration window and had our passports stamped, then headed over to Interpol to get our car's temporary import permit stamped. It should all have been so easy. Unfortunately, sometimes life throws you a curve ball. In this case, it was two over-zealous Interpol agents who wanted a bribe.

We passed them all Missy's documentation, including the temporary import permit stamped by Interpol at the Beit Bridge border post. They then asked for the police clearance certificate which we didn't have. They had only stamped the permit at Beit Bridge, they had not issued us with a separate police clearance certificate. With a sinking feeling, I realised that our good luck at border posts was going to come to an abrupt end. The two Interpol agents said that they'd have to inspect the car and check the engine number to make sure we hadn't stolen it in Zimbabwe. It didn't take a rocket scientist to figure out what was going to happen next. I knew that there was going to be a problem, because Missy had a reconditioned Toyota engine and not the original Mitsubishi Pajero engine. The minute they saw that the engine number was no longer the original, things got nasty. One of them turned to me and asked me what we should do about the situation, obviously his way of asking for a bribe. There was no way in hell I was going to pay a bribe. "It has a reconditioned engine, so obviously it won't have the same engine number," I said struggling to keep a tone of annoyance out of my voice. I knew that getting angry or annoyed wouldn't help matters at all. By this stage, we had attracted a little crowd of onlookers.

"Where is your brake fluid?" one asked with a snarl. "I want to take your brake fluid."

"What are you doing?" I asked with concern.

He growled at me and flung a dirty rag at me. "Clean the engine yourself then." I tried to reach to wear he was pointing on the engine block, but my arm wasn't long enough.

"If you take out our brake fluid, then it's dangerous for us, our brakes won't work." Siobhan sounded very anxious. I could see she was scared as her eyes were big with fright. The Interpol agent snatched the dirty rag out of my hand and stuffed it into Siobhan's hands with such force that she stumbled backwards.

"You so smart, you clean the engine then!"

Siobhan looked as if she was going to start crying. "Leave her alone," I ordered, "She's only fourteen, stop picking on her." The two men mumbled together in a language I didn't understand. "I want to talk to your supervisor now," I said. "Get him on the phone." By now it was getting closer to five o'clock the time when the border closed. We had already been there for 45 minutes. He called his supervisor who said that the car had to be impounded and that we had to return to the police station on the Zimbabwe side of the border.

"The supervisor says you have to give me a lift to the Chirundu Police Station. I must go with you so you don't escape."

I turned to look at a car filled to the brim with our possessions. "There's no space for you," I said simply.

"Did I say you had to empty your car!" He shouted. Things were starting to get nasty, and for the first time I started to feel frightened.

"Well, I'm not leaving my daughter behind to take you," I stated with a far more firm tone than I meant.

"Did I ask you to leave your daughter behind?" He stepped right in front of me, invading my personal space. All this time the second agent was talking on his Blackberry. Amazing how he could afford a mobile phone like that.

I sighed loudly. Things were starting to get a bit out of hand. The agent was getting far too aggressive. "No, you didn't say I had to leave her behind, but I am exploring all the options we have at the moment." He backed down, stepped away from me and said they would make a plan and left. The border closed and we were stranded in no-man's land. We had our exit stamps put into our passport, so we'd effectively left Zimbabwe, but did not have entrance stamps for Zambia. We were stuck. At 6.15pm, the Interpol agents finally returned with a car and said we had to follow them to the Chirundu Police Station.

The police station involved more sitting around and waiting. More border offenders were brought in, some crying inconsolably. The Assistant Interpol Supervisor finally arrived. I hoped he'd see the stupidity of the situation. I'd been in Zimbabwe for two nights and three days. How on earth would I have had time to steal an engine, remove my car's engine and then put a stolen engine in, and at the same time change my car's whole system from diesel to petrol! One look at the expression on the face of the Assistant Supervisor told me that I wouldn't be getting much sympathy from him. He was obviously very annoyed that he had been called in during dinner time!

"You wanted to see me," he snarled, "So I'm here. Not that I can think of any reason why I had to be called in at this time. We take your car and your stuff, and you can go. Goodbye," he laughed and started walking towards the door.

"Wait," I called, "We can't leave our car. All our stuff is in the car!"

His smile reminded me of a crocodile's. "Well in that case, you are impounded with the car. I arrest the car, and with it I arrest you."

I couldn't believe this nightmare was actually happening to us. I thought about options. "I'd like to call the South African Embassy please. I know my rights. I want to call the embassy."

"No," he said turning around at the door. "No embassy, no phone calls. Nobody can help you. You have a stolen engine until you prove otherwise. Anyway, the phone lines are down. They have been for some time. Surrender your keys to the officer." And he left.

The Interpol agent who had been so aggressive earlier on, seemed to have a change of attitude. This aggression was replaced with concern. I'm not sure if it was because Siobhan was crying or if it was the mention of the South African Embassy. But, he went with us into the police station to fill in the arrest report and showed us where to park the car so it'd be safe. "Don't worry, we'll sort it all out in the morning." He introduced us to Inspector Vimbe who was in charge of the station.

Inspector Vimbe, almost as round as he was tall, was very friendly and had a lovely smiling happy face. A sharp contrast to the sullen aggressive looks we'd been subjected to so far. He wanted us to sleep on the floor in the charge office, as he said if we slept in the cells we'd cry all night and upset the other prisoners. The floor of the charge office was filthy, so I said that was not an option. Then he offered us an empty room, but when Siobhan saw cockroaches scuttling around

108

in the corners, she refused to set foot in it. Finally, he relented and said we could sleep in our car, and in that way we could also keep an eye on all our stuff. He promised us that we could use the police toilet during the night. What he didn't tell us at the time, was that the police toilet was in the village near the police station.

We couldn't listen to music because they'd taken the keys to the car. We couldn't open the electric windows either. We couldn't lock the car if we went to the toilet, as we wouldn't be able to unlock it when we returned. The situation was beginning to feel a little desperate. Being impounded with the car was not proving to be fun at all. By this stage, Siobhan needed the toilet badly and she headed into the police station to use the toilet. The uniformed officer was not very friendly. At first he ignored her and then asked her what she wanted in the charge office. She timidly explained that she needed to use the bathroom. Without looking up from his newspaper, he told her the toilet was in the village next door. Siobhan ran back to the car in tears. There was no way she was going to walk into a strange village to search for a toilet in the dark. I left her in the car sobbing and went back into the police station, and stormed down the passage until I found Inspector Vimbe sitting in his office. "This is not on!" I shouted. "This is an infringement on our basic human right to use the toilet." The uniformed officer from the charge office had dropped his newspaper and followed me down the passage to Inspector Vimbe. I turned to face him as he made to grab me from behind. "And you?" I asked in anger, "Would you let your fourteen year old daughter walk through a strange village in the dark looking for a toilet?"

"Yes, I would," he replied with a nasty smile, and it was all I could do not to hit him. We were already in enough trouble as it was, and hitting him might have aggravated the situation.

Inspector Vimbe stood up with a broad smile on his round face, "No problem. We'll escort your daughter to the toilet. No problem in the world is too big for us. Officer, get one of the female prisoners to escort her daughter to the toilet. You see," he smiled again, "No problem is too big for us."

The female prisoner who escorted Siobhan to the bathroom, had been picked up earlier in the day because she no longer looked like her passport photo which had been taken a couple of years earlier. Apparently, when you put in purple and black hair extensions, it changes your appearance so that you are no longer the same person. She was being held in the cells until Interpol managed to get her identity photo which was on file. I dare say, that probably wouldn't look like she did now either. She wasn't upset about her arrest, more resigned to it, as if this sort of thing happened quite frequently in Zimbabwe.

The car was beginning to get stiflingly hot. As the windows couldn't open, no fresh air was coming in. The perspiration was dripping down our necks. It was going to be a hot and uncomfortable night. "Have all the baboons gone?" Siobhan asked peering into the dark. Earlier on, the parking area in front of the police station had been full of large baboons with big yellow teeth.

"Yep, seems that way. Why?" I was beginning to get a cramp in my back.

"I'm going to die if I don't get some air. Think we can open the car doors?" Without waiting for my reply, Siobhan opened her door and breathed in the fresh air. I followed suit and opened my door. No sooner had we opened our doors, than Inspector Vimbe came scuttling towards us waving his arms in the air, his uniform buttons looking ready to pop.

"No! No! Close the doors, you can't leave them open!" He shouted out of breath, the run having taken a lot out of him. "You can't sleep with the doors open. The lion, elephant, hyena all come here at night. They will eat you!"

"We can't sleep with them closed," I explained, "Because then newspaper headlines will read 'FOREIGN TOURISTS SUFFOCATE TO DEATH IN IMPOUNDED CAR IN CHIRUNDU.'

"Open the window a little bit," the good inspector instructed.

"We can't. The car has electric windows and you have our keys." The inspector looked confused as he decided what to do next. "And seeing that you denied me my right to contact my embassy, imagine what would be said then when the headlines read 'MOTHER AND DAUGHTER EATEN BY LIONS AT CHIRUNDU.' They'll investigate what happened and will find out you refused to allow us access to our embassy. Tsk...tsk." Okay I admit it. Sitting in the car in the dark with nothing to do was boring and winding the inspector up was entertaining. Even in the dark you could see the expressions changing on his face as he puzzled over what he should do.

"Okay, okay. This is what we'll do." He licked his lips nervously. I don't think he actually had the authority to do what he was going to do. "You see the motel there across the road? Maybe it would be better if you spent the night there, and then came back early in the morning in time to see us change guard."

I looked at the motel peeping out behind the long line of trucks. "We're not walking there alone. It's dangerous." I aimed to make it as difficult as possible, so they'd think twice about arresting tourists in the future.

"Okay, okay. I'll get another officer and we'll walk you to the motel. We'll even carry your bags for you." On the way to the motel Vimbe was very chatty, asking us about our trip. He noticed the copy of my book 'Not Telling' Siobhan was carrying and asked to have a look at it. "I like to read. Maybe I should move to Tanzania so I can carry your bags there," he joked. He wasn't a bad guy actually, definitely much better than the other overflowing-with-testosterone types in Interpol.

"So, are the Zimbabwe Police paying for our motel and buying us dinner?" I asked wishfully, knowing what the answer would be.

"The Zimbabwe Police Department has no money. But maybe you can buy us a drink?"

I shook my head sadly. "You've go to be kidding me!" After all that had happened I had to buy them a drink? We said goodbye and sent them on their way, contacted room service and ordered the most delicious beef stew and sadza. We were too wired to go and sleep, even though it was quite late, so we read a bit, looked at our photos and videos from our trip so far and felt much better.

The motel was actually one of the nicer places we'd stayed in; just $30 a night for a triple room, decent bathroom and comfortable beds. Breakfast was not included.

Close to **Chirundu**, just off the road to Lusaka are 50 000 year old fossilised trees from the Karoo Period.

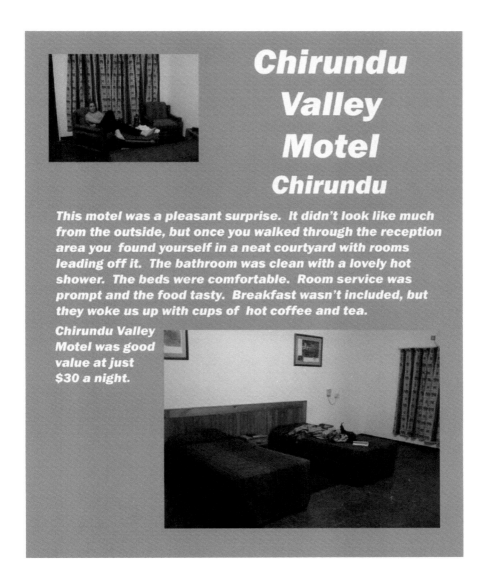

Chirundu Valley Motel
Chirundu

This motel was a pleasant surprise. It didn't look like much from the outside, but once you walked through the reception area you found yourself in a neat courtyard with rooms leading off it. The bathroom was clean with a lovely hot shower. The beds were comfortable. Room service was prompt and the food tasty. Breakfast wasn't included, but they woke us up with cups of hot coffee and tea.

Chirundu Valley Motel was good value at just $30 a night.

Stats for the day					
Odometer Start	Odometer Finish	Day's Kilometres	Depart Time	Arrive Time	Hours travel
186702	187115	413	11h30	16h15	4 and three quarter hours
Fuel	Cost local currency	Cost US$	Accommodation	Cost local currency	Cost US$
82.18 litres	$101.90	$101.90	Chirundu Valley Motel	$30	$30

ZAMBIA

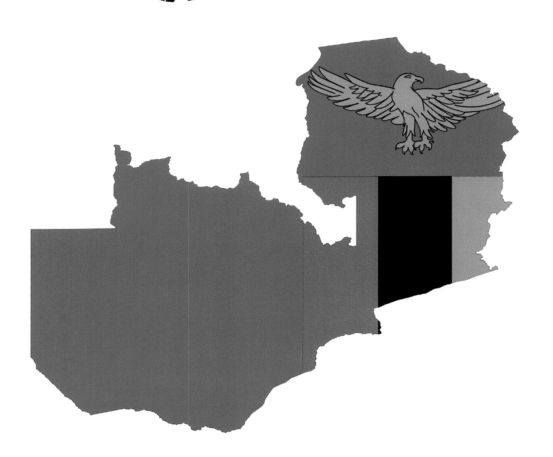

Surprisingly enough, both Siobhan and I slept like the dead. We were woken up by a knock on the door and a tray with hot tea and coffee. No toast though; I guess that would have been stretching it. We weren't in a rush to head over to the police station. The chances of them having verified that my car engine wasn't stolen was very slim. Bureaucracy tends to work at a very slow place in Africa, and Zimbabwe was no exception. We had a lovely hot shower and ate an orange each for breakfast. Luckily, we still had oranges left from the big bag of them I'd bought when we left Pretoria. They were coming in very useful. After fiddling around with the TV channels, we decided that there was nothing interesting to watch so we may as well head over to the police station. We packed our dirty clothes in the carrier bags and walked past the big trucks blocking the road to the border and big troops of huge hairy baboons that were foraging for leftovers in piles of rubbish.

The policeman on duty was another aggressive type overflowing with testosterone. He refused to give me our car keys so that we could put our stuff away. I'm not sure where he expected us to go or wait, but he wasn't very impressed when we sat down on the benches in the charge office. "What you want here? Wait outside," and he waved his hand as if to dismiss us. I looked at the troops of baboons running around outside and the lack of outdoor seating arrangements and decided to stay sitting where I was. I continued to stare at the duty policeman who was beginning to feel uncomfortable. "Go, go," he kept repeating every time he caught my gaze. I wish we could go, but without the car and no more cash on me, we had nowhere to go. There definitely would not be an ATM in Chirundu, and if there was, I seriously doubted it would take a foreign visa card. After about twenty minutes of my penetrating stare, the poor policeman eventually went to ask his superior if we could have our keys back to put our stuff back in the car. My fierce stare had definitely reduced his testosterone levels and diminished his aggression. He gave us the keys. "Just put stuff in and bring back keys right away, okay?" I nodded my head in agreement, having no intention whatsoever of returning the keys.

The night before I had turned on the car alarm before we left for the motel. It was a sneaky move on my part, but with all our belongings in the car, I wanted there to be a deterrent just in case. It's not that I didn't trust the police, but my car's contents were quite tempting. I had asked them to give me a receipt for my car and contents, so that if anything went missing I could sue them. They had refused but they did get the message not to mess with my car. The alarm was just an extra on my part. However, when we got to the car we noticed that the alarm had been turned off. Someone had been in the car, but a quick check showed that nothing was missing.

We quickly found a hole in the mound of goods at the back to put the bag with our dirty clothes in, and then settled down in the front seats for the wait. We knew it would be a long wait. Our punishment for not paying a bribe. Hearing shouting from behind the car, I checked my side-view mirror and saw that the policeman who had given us the keys was leaning out the window of the charge office. "I want my keys! Give me my keys! I lock you in jail! Give me my keys!" By this time, Siobhan and I were beyond caring and we just ignored his pleas for the keys. I read a book and Siobhan played around with the camera and took photos of herself - as you do when you are incarcerated in your car with nothing much else to do.

A knock on my window interrupted my reading. A young man introduced himself as an Interpol agent. He was nice and pleasant, a huge contrast to the specimens who had 'arrested' us the day before. He asked if he could look at the engine number again, so I lifted the bonnet and he wrote down the number on a scrap piece of paper. He said he was going to contact Interpol in Harare, and we should be able to leave quite soon. I smiled and thanked him, seriously doubting that we would be going anywhere soon. An hour later the Senior Interpol agent knocked on the window and introduced himself. He was also friendly and pleasant, chatted to us about our trip and apologised profusely for the inconvenience caused. He explained that they were also inconvenienced by this, as the phone lines to Harare appeared to be down. A half hour after he left, Inspector Vimbe, the jolly officer from the night before, knocked on the window. He asked us if we had slept well and then asked if we could give him a copy of my book, Not Telling. He wanted an autographed copy of my book. I fished a copy out of my bag; luckily I had a spare, and he said he'd be thinking of me when he read it. I wasn't sure I quite liked that idea, but I guess whatever floats his boat - as long as we were left alone and would eventually be able to leave Chrirundu. No sooner had he left, then the Interpol agent returned. "I've finally managed to contact Harare, sorry for the delay, our systems are terrible here. Their power's off in Harare at the moment, so they can't go on the internet to verify your engine number, but they are sure the problem will be solved shortly and I have to phone them back in 45 minutes. I told them to hurry up and sort this as you have a long road ahead." The 45 minutes stretched to three hours. Nobody came near us or asked for us to return the keys. It seemed as if we'd been forgotten.

At 11.30am Vimbe came out again. "We haven't actually arrested you; we arrested your vehicle with you in it!" he laughed. Obviously that was very amusing to him. I gave a grim smile. It wasn't very amusing to me. Vimbe turned serious. He spoke to us about God and the power of prayer. "We've been trying to call Harare but they are not answering the phone. You have to start praying now, that's all that can help you. Maybe when the sun is a little higher, and you have prayed a bit, the phone in Harare will work."

At 12h30 the Interpol agent returned. "I got through! Your engine is verified! You didn't steal it, it was a reconditioned one from Tanzania! You may go, just let me sign this paper and give it to the Interpol agents at the border post." No shit Sherlock! That's exactly what I had been telling them all along.

The Interpol agents at the border were the same ones who had apprehended us the day before. They stared at me with blank looks and stamped all the forms. It was only when I looked at the temporary export permit from Tanzania, that I saw that the new reconditioned engine number was there. They had ignored that piece of paper, refusing to look at it. If they had studied it, they would have seen that that engine was registered in Tanzania. A whole wasted day would have been avoided. Bastards!

We had no problems on the Zambian side of the building. We didn't have to pay carbon tax or the road toll as our papers from the last time we drove through Zambia were still valid. All in all, it took us one hour to get through both borders.

We drove to Lusaka in a bit of a mind fog. The three hours it took to get there passed so quickly. The ordeal at Chirundu had taken quite a lot out of us and we felt quite flat. Initially, we'd wanted to stop half-way between Lusaka and the Malawi border, but we were too tired and hungry to travel any further. An orange at 6.30 in the morning just doesn't fill you up! We stopped at the Downtown Shopping Centre just before the Kafue roundabout; drew money from an ATM, found the bathroom and ordered huge helpings of delicious butter chicken from Jalapeno's. The helpings were so huge, that hungry as we were there was no way we could finish them. We had them pack them up as take-aways; it'd be perfect for dinner.

Siobhan studied the map and directed us to the road to Malawi. It was quite easy to find, and a little way out of Lusaka we started seeing signs for hotels and motels. One name stood out from the rest, the Comfort Lodge. We felt that we needed a bit of comfort after our harrowing experience and turned in there.

The room was perfect, they had cable TV and wireless internet. We were sorted and could finally relax.

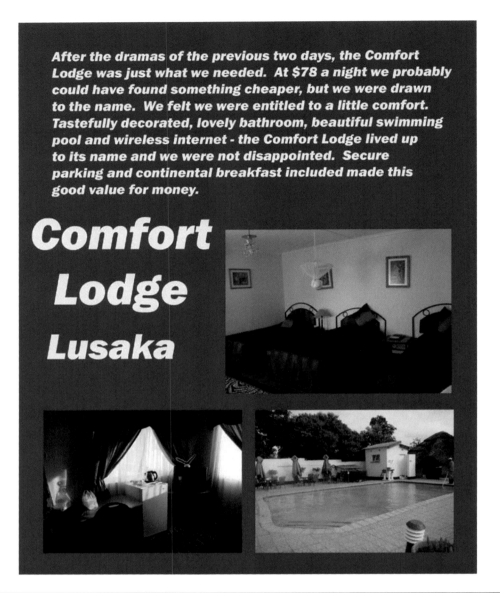

After the dramas of the previous two days, the Comfort Lodge was just what we needed. At $78 a night we probably could have found something cheaper, but we were drawn to the name. We felt we were entitled to a little comfort. Tastefully decorated, lovely bathroom, beautiful swimming pool and wireless internet - the Comfort Lodge lived up to its name and we were not disappointed. Secure parking and continental breakfast included made this good value for money.

Comfort Lodge Lusaka

Stats for the day					
Odometer Start	Odometer Finish	Day's Kilometres	Depart Time	Arrive Time	Hours travel
187115	187268	153	13h30	16h30	3 hours
Fuel	Cost local currency	Cost US$	Accommodation	Cost local currency	Cost US$
0	0	0	Comfort Lodge	400000 kwacha	$77.97

The **South Luangwa National Park** is in eastern Zambia in the valley of the Luangwa River. It is a world-renowned wildlife haven and supports large populations of Thornicroft's Giraffe, and herds of elephant and buffalo. The Luangwa River itself supports a large number of crocodiles and hippos. It is one of the best-known national parks in Africa for walking safaris. The park covers 9,050 km² and spans two ecoregions, Patches of flooded grassland habitats (floodplains) are found close to the river, on which hippopotamus graze at night. Their dung released into the river fertilises its waters and sustains the fish population which in turn sustains the crocodiles.

After toast and coffee, we said farewell to the Comfort Lodge and hit the road at 8.30am. We drove past some fuel stations, thinking we could refuel a bit later. My son used to have a T-shirt he'd bought in Thailand with a picture of a monkey, a chainsaw, and the monkey's paw lying on the ground. The caption read, 'Slow Learner.' I need to get myself a T-shirt with a picture of a car stranded on the side of the road and a signpost saying next fuel station 200km ahead, along with the 'Slow Learner' caption. I have no idea why I cause myself so much stress, and why I don't fill up the car when I see a fuel station. What makes me say, "We'll stop in the next town," I'll never know. Especially when I've never driven along the road before and have no idea how far away the next town is and if they even have a fuel station. It's just crazy, but I do it time and time again. This day of course was no exception, but to make matters worse, not only did I need to find a town with a fuel station, but the town had to have an ATM as well. As my fuel gauge dropped lower and lower, and each town we passed got smaller and smaller, the likelihood of finding an ATM grew less realistic. I had a sinking feeling we were going to be stranded on the side of the road without fuel or money. Not a great combination in any country. We stopped at a BP Garage in Nyimba, and tried to persuade the pump attendant to take US$ instead of Kwacha. Unfortunately, she wasn't buying it. It had to be Kwacha or we couldn't get fuel. Just as I leaned against the car thinking of a Plan A and a Plan B, wondering what we could sell to get some Kwacha, a flash of turquoisy-blue caught my eye. Lo and behold, there before me on the side of the fuel station was a Barclays Bank ATM! I could not believe my luck! The angels were definitely looking after us!

The area we'd driven through up to Nyimba, was supposed to be one of the richest wildlife areas in Zambia. Other than a few troops of baboons, we'd seen nothing. The road to Nyimba was in very good condition; after Nyimba it deteriorated rapidly with potholes breaking up the tar. But as bad as it was, the potholes were not as bad as they were up north. They did still manage to knock my exhaust system loose though, and poor Missy started to sound like a tractor running on dirty fuel.

RECIPES FROM AFRICA – Zambia

Microwave NshimaRecipe for 3-4 people
Ingredients
1 cup maize meal
2 cups boiling water
1 tablespoon butter
Salt to taste
Method
Pour the boiling water into a large microwave proof bowl. Dissolve the salt in the water. Slowly add the maize meal to the water, stirring all the while. Add the butter. Microwave on high for 3 minutes. Take it out and give it a decent stir. The nshima should be starting to thicken nicely. Microwave again for another 3 minutes. Take it out and stir it, adding a little more water if necessary. Cover with a lid and do a few more 3 minute sessions, followed by a quick stir and more water if necessary. As soon as it resembles mashed potato it is done. Leave the bowl to stand for about 2 minutes with the lid on before you serve the nshima.

By the time we reached Petauke we were quite ravenous, and stopped at Chimwemwe Lodge for lunch. The lodge is situated 400km east of Lusaka and has 20 self-contained chalets and a great restaurant. Definitely a place to stop off at in the future. The executive suites were only $50 a night, the hostel under $20 a night and the meals were tasty and reasonably priced. Luxury at a bargain price.

Siobhan tried to convince me to stop the car and catch one of the little black pigs which were wandering around on the side of the road. The fact that we had nowhere to put it or that we would have to smuggle it across several borders did not seem to faze her. She wanted one as a pet to keep in her room as it was "so cute!" All I could think of, were the difficulties of house-training it.

We arrived at Chipata on the Zambian/ Malawi border at 5pm, too late to go through. Siobhan had ear-marked a guesthouse called Mama Rulas, but despite her great directions, we couldn't find it. As it turned out, we didn't drive far enough down the road, and having had enough driving for the day, checked into the Chipata Motel. We were greeted by the chef who also showed us to our room and took our dinner order. The room was okay, nothing to get excited about, and the hot water didn't work. At just under $30 a night including continental breakfast, it did the job and one couldn't complain.

Chipata Motel
Chipata

The rooms were basic and comfortable. The hot water didn't work in the bathroom. The continental breakfast consisted of a cup of coffee and a slice of bread with butter. They didn't have jam. Not bad for just under $30 a night.

Stats for the day					
Odometer Start	**Odometer Finish**	**Day's Kilometres**	**Depart Time**	**Arrive Time**	**Hours travel**
187268	187868	600	08h30	17h00	8 and a half hours
Fuel	**Cost local currency**	**Cost US$**	**Accommodation**	**Cost local currency**	**Cost US$**
76.91 litres	600000 kwacha	$116.96	Chipata Motel	150000 kwacha	$29.24

121

Despite the happy chef promising us faithfully that there'd be jam with our continental breakfast, there wasn't. Two thick slices of home-made bread, a scraping of butter and a choice of coffee or Milo was the Chipata Motel's variation of what constituted a continental breakfast. I'd always imagined continental breakfasts to be fresh fruit, coffee, cheese, jam and croissants. After this trip, I needed to change my mental picture of a continental breakfast. At least when I am in Africa.

Chipata has ATMs and a Shoprite Centre, so we were able to draw some more money to fill the fuel tank and buy some snacks for the road. The Malawi border is only 24km from Chipata.

RECIPES FROM AFRICA - Zambia

Nkuku

This easy to make chicken dish is great to put in a pot and forget about while you plan your next holiday. It serves 8-10 people.

Ingredients

3kg chicken

½ cup cooking oil

1 large onion coarsely chopped

2 large tomatoes cubed

Optional kalembula (sweet potato leaves) or something else resembling spinach

2 cups water

1 red chilli finely chopped

1 jar peanut butter

Salt and pepper to taste

Method

Cut the chicken into portions and season with salt and pepper. Heat the oil and cook the chicken until brown. Add in the coarsely chopped onion. Stir in the tomatoes and leafy vegetables. Mix well. Add the water and turn down the heat, letting it all simmer for about 30 minutes. Empty the jar of peanut butter into a small bowl and add enough boiling water so that you make a smooth runny paste. Add your peanut butter paste and chopped chilli to your pot of chicken stew. Mix well and let it simmer for another 20 minutes. Serve hot with rice or maize meal porridge.

We reached the border at 9.15am and sailed through both the Zambian and Malawian sides without any problems. We managed to change $40 for Malawi Kwacha with the touts on the Zambian side. At the Malwian side we had to pay a 1200 Malwawi Kwacha border fee, but that was it. For some reason I had expected Malawi to be far more developed than it was. I'm not sure where I got that idea from, but in reality it was the least developed country we travelled through. There were hardly any cars on the road, most people seemed to walk everywhere and the villages we passed were just groups of huts.

The road was actually in good condition and we were able to travel quite fast and make good time. Lilongwe, the capital city, is just 124km from the border. The signs on the road were visible and we drove through Lilongwe without stopping and headed out to Salima which was near Lake Malawi. We'd heard quite a bit about the beauty of the lake and were keen to see it. Our internet research showed that Malawi was very small and all towns were quite close to each other. In actual fact, the distances between the big towns was far greater than was given on the internet. Our plan was to draw money in Salima, drive through to Senga Bay to have lunch, then Nkhata Bay to spend the night. Unfortunately, the best laid plans often hit hidden snags. This time it wasn't a lack of fuel at the fuel station or a lack of ATM machines, it was that my ATM card decided to give up the ghost.

It's hard to describe the feeling when you put your card into a machine in a strange country, knowing you don't have any cash on you, and you get an error message. At first it's disbelief, then panic, then red hot rage. None of these feelings put money in your wallet however. We tried three different banks in Salima, then drove to Senga Bay but there weren't any ATMs there, so headed back to Salima. I still had fuel, but doubted that it would be enough to get us to Nkhata Bay. We tried the ATMs again, but still had no joy. Eventually we tracked down an internet cafe. I thought I might be able to Skype my bank, but the internet was down. It had been down for the past few days. I wondered if that was why my ATM card couldn't work. I drove around wondering what to do, bought a phonecard and went back to the internet cafe and phoned my bank. They said that there wasn't a problem with my card but a problem with the ATM machines. We decided to forgo lunch and rather use my remaining Malawi Kwacha to put in more fuel. Unfortunately, I think we got cheated. At the time I was filling up, a local woman was waiting to get a plastic container filled with petrol. I went to the bathroom and by the time I got back the woman had gone. Siobhan was busy reading and hadn't seen anything. But suffice to say, I had to pay for 25 litres of petrol and my fuel gauge hadn't moved a centimetre.

As we were leaving Salima, I saw the most bizarre sight. A human haystack was running straight towards us and as it passed them, the locals scattered and looked away. 5 minutes later, we passed two men with straw skirts and masks and their bodies painted in stripes. Obviously, they were dressed for some kind of a ceremonial dance. We later found out that these were Nyau dancers, a tradition amongst the Chewa people.

There are numerous mysterious tales of how the **Nyau dancers** of the Chewa people use their powers on anyone they lay hands on. The dance itself is said to involve witchcraft and is shrouded in secrecy. There are different nyau dancers. They appear at different occasions like weddings, funerals, inauguration of chiefs, initiation ceremonies, etc. They alledgedly sleep in graveyards. The costumes they wear depends on whether the nyau dancer is for the purpose of creating fear or entertainment. The nyau costume consists of a mask, birds'feathers and animal skin on rest of the head. Usually the rest of the body isn't covered except between the waist and the knees. A wrap like skirt made of strips of animal skins or cloth is used to cover this part of the body. The nyau also wears bells around his ankles, which are either made of metal or from a type of seed pod dried hard and filled with stones. The costume is designed to hide the identity of the nyau dancer. They also change their voice to a guttural sound when speaking, so that even their wife may not recognize them. Nyau dancers whose role is to create fear tend to cover their bodies completely to avoid recognition. Young boys join the nyau group to learn life skills required for adult married life. To graduate and become an adult they have to learn the nyau dance. Only if they have mastered the dance, will young Chewa men be allowed to get marriage. After graduation, a few dancers are retained in the nyau group to continue the traditions.

We drove the 104km to Nkhotakota, hoping against all hope that there'd be a functioning ATM there. The map showed Nkhotakota to be a big town. After driving around there, we decided that there wasn't an ATM in Nkotakota. If there was, we sure as hell couldn't find it. The fuel tank was on empty, and all we could do was try and drive the 54km to Dwangwa and hope we had better luck there. We had wasted over three hours trying to get my card to work and find an ATM, so we knew that there was no way we'd make it to Nkhata Bay.

20km from Dwangwa, the fuel light came on. I hoped we'd just be able to make it to Dwangwa and hopefully, an ATM. Inside I was feeling desperate. Outwardly, I managed to maintain my good cheer.

Somehow or other we managed to reach Dwangwa just as dusk set in. The ATM machines we tried rejected my card. Somebody suggested we try the ATM machine at the Standard Bank on the sugar plantation. It was a way out of town and by this time my nerves were shot. I didn't hold out much hope as my ATM card didn't work in Standard Bank ATMs in South Africa. My mind was working overtime, trying to come up with Plans B, C and D, as my plan A had just failed. After what seemed like ages, we arrived at the Standard Bank in the middle of the sugar plantation. The air smelled quite bad; I recognised the same smell from wineries I'd visited in the past. Besides Ilovo syrup, they also make cane spirits. I was initially quite hopeful when the ATM managed to read my card and my name came up on the screen. This was soon dashed when the ATM only dispensed me 200 Malawi Kwacha at a time. As my bank card is a UK one, each transaction was costing me a two pound transaction fee. Dejected and depressed, I sat down on the bank steps debating what to do next. I had no more money for phone cards to call my bank; no fuel in the car; knew nobody in Malawi; had no place to stay and it was dark. The situation seemed a little desperate. Siobhan was unconcerned. "You always make a plan and it always turns out alright, so I don't know what you're worried about." It was difficult to think of a cunning plan at night in a strange country.

The man who had been waiting to use the ATM after me, approached. "Try the Kasasa Club. I'm sure they'll help you. It belongs to this sugar plantation." He pointed far in the distance to where I'd find the clubhouse. I hoped I'd have enough fuel to get there.

The clubhouse was packed. There was a big golf tournament on, and people had come from all over Malawi to take part. Probably not the best time of the year to ask if they had two spare beds. After hearing my sad story, the manager said he'd make a plan and put us up in a house for the night, the guests booked in there had called to say they'd only be arriving the next morning. The manager took my camera as security, and said we'd sort something out in the morning.

All night I tossed and turned trying to work out what we could do to get out of this tricky situation. Each time I turned, the bed made a strange noise. Like wood tearing. At 2am, the bed completely collapsed. These people had helped us and I'd broken their bed. I moved into the other bedroom and went to sleep, keeping any movement to a minimum.

Kasasa Club Dwangwa

The Kasasa Club is on a big sugar plantation next to the golf course. The accommodation is in self-contained houses. The club house has a good restuarant and bar. A full English Breakfast was included in the $73 a night room rate.

Stats for the day					
Odometer Start	Odometer Finish	Day's Kilometres	Depart Time	Arrive Time	Hours travel
187868	188360	492	10h00	19h00	9 hours
Fuel	Cost local currency	Cost US$	Accommodation	Cost local currency	Cost US$
63.54 litres	350000 zk 6500 mk	$111.61	Kasasa Club	11000 mk	$73.43

Day Ten: Dwangwa to Mbeya

This might be day ten of the up trip, but it was day five of wearing the same socks. My plan of sorting each day's clothes into piles and putting each pile into a plastic packet to bring out at each stop had backfired when I'd forgotten to include socks in the piles. After a restless night of broken beds and serious thinking, I drew myself a hot bath and lay soaking while I formulated a plan. Sometime during the night, I had decided to discard all other plans and just focus on perfecting one plan. The plan was to ask to see the big boss, the general manager. He'd be making an appearance for the golf tournament, and then I would ask him whether they could fill my car's tank with petrol. I'd pay for the accommodation and fuel when I arrived back in Tanzania. It would mean travelling through Malawi with no cash at all, but I'd calculated that a full tank should get me to the border. We'd been looking forward to spending a couple of days at Nkhata Bay, but that's life. It just meant we'd have to return some day.

When we went to ask for the general manager we received a pleasant surprise. "Go to the dining room and have a good breakfast while you wait for him to arrive. A full English breakfast is included in your room rate." We had the works: cereal, yoghurt, eggs, bacon, sausage, toast, endless cups of coffee, juice. We consumed so much we both felt quite ill. We'd hardly eaten the day before, and didn't know when we'd have money to eat again. I suppose stuffing ourselves was quite natural under the circumstances.

The general manager was a fellow South African, and readily agreed to my plan. He was quite concerned whether or not we'd manage to reach the border on one tank though. They gave us back our camera and escorted us to the fuel station in town where they filled the tank, rocking the car so that we could get in extra fuel. Every drop would count. We finally left Dwangwa at 9.20am, ready to drive the 140km to Nkhata bay. It was going to be touch and go whether we made the border before it closed for the night.

The glimpses of the lake and in general, the Malawi scenery was quite spectacular. The road next to the lake is quite winding and narrow. There are lots of small rivers and many bridges which allow only one vehicle to cross at a time. We were stopped at a few road blocks, but the police were very friendly. All were in awe of the distance we'd driven and still had to drive. Maybe this impressed them so much, that they never asked for any papers or gave us any grief. One even wanted to marry Siobhan. He said he could provide a nice hut for her to live in. Siobhan pursed her lips and stared out her window, refusing to make eye contact with her would-be suitor. Obviously, his proposal did not impress her at all. Just before reaching Nkhata Bay, we were stopped by a truck full of soldiers with guns. The soldier in charge brought his gun with him as he came to my

128

window. Peering in, he said, "Hmm, no room for you to transport one of my soldiers to the next town."

"No room, sorry," I smiled not feeling sorry at all. Somehow, I didn't fancy having a man with a large gun travelling with me in the car, even if he was a soldier. I carried on with the journey, drove up a large hill and there before us was Nkhata Bay. Nkhata Bay was stunningly beautiful. A rustic village next to the lake.

At Nkhata Bay we found a backpackers we'd definitely have stayed in if we had managed to get my bank card to work in the ATMs. The Big Blue Backpackers had a vibe like none other we'd encountered anywhere on our trip so far. Definitely a place to recommend and come back to. You can check out their website www.bigbluestarbackpackers.com or email the owner for more information bigbluestarbackpackers@gmail.com. We found their rates to be well within our budget - if we had hac money. Camping is 500 MK per person; the 11 bed dorm is 700 MK per person; the 4 bed dorm is 900 MK per person; the single chalet is 1500 MK per room and the double bed chalet is 2500 MK per room. In addition, there's free wireless internet, free snorkelling and canoeing, DSTV, a DVD library to borrow from and a book swap. We saw advertised on the board that there was a pub quiz for that night. Next door to the Big Blue Backpackers is the Aqua Afrika Dive School which offers diving courses for as little as $350! We cannot recommend this place highly enough.

The owner outside one of the chalets.

We left Nkhata Bay at 12 noon and thought it wouldn't take too long to get to Mzunzu, the next town, as it was only 45km away. How wrong we were! The steep ascent and winding roads littered with potholes took their toll on our time, as Missy struggled to make it up some of the steeper inclines. The bonus was that, as we were forced to travel so slowly, we got to appreciate and enjoy the amazing views. From Mzunzu, the 220km road to Karonga was in much better shape, and there were times when we could accelerate to 80-100km per hour.

RECIPES FROM AFRICA - Malawi

Mbatata

This delicious low cost meal is perfect for those on a limited budget or wanting an alternative to lasagne.

4 tablespoons cooking oil; 2 large sweet potatoes, peeled and sliced thinly; 1 bunch spring onions finely chopped
500g minced meat; 4 tomatoes cut into cubes; 1 small tin tomato paste; 1 tablespoon vinegar
Salt and pepper to taste; Breadcrumbs

Cheese Sauce Ingredients

2 tablespoons butter or margarine; 1 tablespoon flour; 1 cup milk; ¼ cup grated cheese

Method

Put 3 tablespoons of the oil in a frying pan and fry the sweet potatoes until golden brown. Remove them and put them on a plate so long until later. Put the last tablespoon of oil into the frying pan, add the onions and fry them until they are soft and translucent. Add the mince and brown it. Add the tomatoes, tomato paste, vinegar and seasoning. Simmer for half an hour. While it's simmering, prepare the cheese sauce. Melt the butter in a saucepan, add the flour and stir until mixed with the butter. Add the milk and stir until it thickens nicely. Add the cheese and mix it in so that it melts. Remove from the heat. Grease a large ovenproof dish and arrange layers of sweet potatoes and the mince mixture as you would a lasagne. Pour the cheese sauce on the top and sprinkle with the breadcrumbs. Bake at 180 degrees Celsius or 350 degrees Fahrenheit for 45 minutes.

RECIPES FROM AFRICA - Malawi

Masamba cakes

This is a fantastic snack to serve while watching sport on the TV or waiting for the meat to cook on the barbecue. So easy to make, you can even get your children to knock these up for you. Serves 8.

Ingredients

1 bunch spinach finely chopped; 1 cup cooked macaroni; 2 eggs; 2 cups breadcrumbs
½ teaspoon sugar; ½ cup cake flour; 4 tablespoons margarine/butter; Salt and pepper to taste
Water; Oil for frying

Method

Boil the spinach until cooked. Mix the cooked macaroni with the spinach. Add 1 of the eggs, half the breadcrumbs, seasoning and sugar. Mix and make flat cakes by hand. In another small bowl, mix the remaining egg with the leftover breadcrumbs. Dip the flat cakes into the flour and then into the egg and breadcrumb mixture. Fry the masamba cakes until cooked through. Serve with a salsa dip or tomato and onion relish.

What slowed us down even more, were the five road blocks we had to stop at. The police were all very friendly; they chatted about the Football World Cup and wished us a safe journey, but with us racing against time to get to the border, it was a pleasant distraction we could have done without. At each road block, we'd ask what our chances were like of making it to the border in time. Some replies were positive; most were negative. Unfortunately, without any money there was no way we could stop somewhere for the night. We just had to make the border! When we reached Karonga, we saw a sign saying that the border was only 45km away, and for the first time, we thought we might make it. Unfortunately, there were two roadwork detours which brought our speed down to about 10km an hour and three large roadblocks, which delayed us considerably. The police at the road blocks said that the border closed at 5pm, and there was no way we would make it.

Siobhan and I made the decision to head to the border anyway, and spend the night there sleeping in the car if need be. The closer we got to the border, the more people we saw, making the road quite congested. There were large groups of people walking, some cycling and others sitting on the road braiding each other's hair which I found quite bizarre. Why would you sit facing oncoming traffic to braid hair?

Hastings Banda, the first president of Malawi, was considered one of Africa's most influential leaders in the last 50 years, yet he was one of the biggest despots and tyrants. He was never seen in public without his trademark black three-piece suits, flywhisk, walking stick, homburg hat and handkerchief. During his time in office, he had a huge 300-room palace, with a school and a supermarket constructed, and amassed a personal fortune estimated at $320 million. In brutality, he was matched by Idi Amin Dada of Uganda. Because of his conservatism, Malawi was one of the last countries to have television, in the 1990s. He is the only African who left his country and stayed out for 42 years but returned to lead it to independence and rule it for 33 years. Banda never married and remained a 'bachelor' till death. Banda presided over a police state where any form of dissent brought sudden death, torture, exile or deportation. Women were not allowed to bare their thighs or wear trousers. Men were banned from growing beards or long hair because it signalled dissent. Like Amin, it is said he murdered his enemies and fed their corpses to crocodiles. In a BBC interview in the early 1990s, he threatened that should Malawian exiles calling for introduction of multipartism return home, he would feed them to crocodiles. Many people thought he was joking, until some rivers dried up in a drought exposing the bones of human skeletons.

We reached the border at 5.10pm and to our surprise it was still open! We passed through Malawi immigration smooth as, and had to wait for the Customs official to clear the car. He was nowhere to be found, and we had some anxious moments thinking we'd be stuck in No-man's-Land if the Tanzanian border closed before we got through. By this time, the bladder problem resurfaced. So while Siobhan waited for the Customs guy to appear, I headed for the toilet, only to find that it was a pay toilet. I had no money. I begged and pleaded for them to let me use the bathroom, but the woman guarding the toilet was adamant. No money, no toilet. I made a big deal of walking away with my legs crossed. I heard laughter behind me but my plan worked. The woman called me back and let me use the bathroom for free. By the time I got back to Customs, the guy had stamped all the necessary papers and we were free to head to the Tanzanian side. The Tanzanian side were about to close but were very friendly, welcoming us home. The official waved the car papers away. "There's no need to see the papers. It's our car and you're bringing it home."

Not once at any of the border posts, did anybody ask about our stuff in the car or ask us to pay duty. We left the Tanzanian border post at 5.50pm to drive the 10km to Mbeya. My plan was to try my ATM card again in Mbeya. If it still didn't work I'd come up with a new plan. My car had just over a quarter of a tank left and I was quite confident it would see us to Mbeya.

What gets me through a bad adventure is the knowledge that for every down there is an up and for every up there is a down.

TANZANIA

    As this was a different road to Mbeya than the one we'd driven on before when we went into Zambia, we were completely unprepared for the steep hills and winding road. It was like driving on a rollercoaster; each hill we encountered was steeper than the one before. Missy really struggled and I had to keep changing down to first gear. The hills never seemed to end. At the last big hill, Missy gave up. She couldn't make it. It was pitch dark and it was the first time Siobhan cried from fear. We'd seen how the trucks hurtled through the night. We were an accident waiting to happen.

Siobhan wanted to get out the car and try and push it up the hill. The car was over-laden and very heavy. There was no way she'd be able to budge it. To make matters worse, the fuel light had come on as Missy chomped through the fuel in her efforts to try and get up the hills. I willed the car up that last hill. Putting on the hazard lights to warn trucks that we were there, I revved the engine and slowly let out the clutch. Missy would move forward a couple of inches and then give up. I'd pull up the hand brake, start the engine and repeat the procedure and slowly, inch by inch, Missy made her way to the top of the hill. By the time we reached the top, my fingers were covered in callouses from clutching the steering wheel so tightly. I think I aged ten years. It was only the next day we found out we'd driven up the side of a dormant volcano.

We free-wheeled down the mountain to save fuel. We made it to Mbeya by the skin of our teeth and tried three ATMs but they all said there was an error. My bank card had definitely stopped working - probably the magnetic strip had been damaged. It was late, we were tired. It had taken us 3 hours to drive the 108km from the border to Mbeya. I drove to the hotel we'd stayed at on our down trip, the Rift Valley Hotel, and checked us in at full board. They remembered us, so they didn't ask for a deposit and I figured I'd make a plan to get money in the morning.

RECIPES FROM AFRICA - Tanzania

Supuya Papai

This unusual soup can be served hot or cold and is guaranteed to make you feel as if you are living in the tropics.

Ingredients

1 medium firm papaya
1 teaspoon butter
1 large onion finely chopped
500ml stock
Salt and pepper to taste
1 cup cream
1 teaspoon fresh chopped chives

Method

1. Peel the papaya and cut it into pieces.
2. Heat the butter and fry the papaya and onion without letting it brown.
3. Add the stock and seasoning and let it simmer until the papaya is soft.
4. Pour everything into a blender and blend it until smooth.
5. Add half the cream and mix it in thoroughly.
6. If serving cold, put it in the fridge to get cold and pour on the remainder of the cream and sprinkle the chopped chives on as a decoration just before serving.
7. If serving hot, pour the mixture from the blender back into the pot and simmer until hot.
8. Add the rest of the cream and sprinkle on the chives before serving.

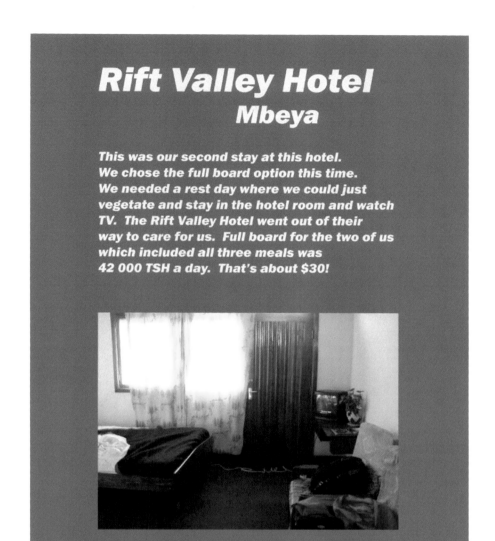

Rift Valley Hotel
Mbeya

*This was our second stay at this hotel.
We chose the full board option this time.
We needed a rest day where we could just
vegetate and stay in the hotel room and watch
TV. The Rift Valley Hotel went out of their
way to care for us. Full board for the two of us
which included all three meals was
42 000 TSH a day. That's about $30!*

Stats for the day					
Odometer Start	**Odometer Finish**	**Day's Kilometres**	**Depart Time**	**Arrive Time**	**Hours travel**
188360	188955	595km	09h20	21h30	12 hours and 10 minutes
Fuel	**Cost local currency**	**Cost US$**	**Accommodation**	**Cost local currency**	**Cost US$**
86.85 litres	22251 mk	$148.54	Rift Valley Hotel	30000 TSH	$19.93

We were stranded. It was a Sunday and my bank in the UK could not help us until the Monday. They said I'd probably need a new ATM card. I contacted a friend in Moshi who said he'd sort something out the Monday morning first thing. All we could do, was make the most of our relaxation time. We couldn't drive anywhere and explore the town as we had not a drop of fuel left. The night before's struggle up the volcanic cones had completely depleted the fuel supply. Food was taken care of, as we'd opted for paying the extra $10 a day for full board. We did make sure, to put in our lunch order and dinner order in the morning though, so we wouldn't have to wait so long for a meal as we'd done the last time we'd stayed there.

The day dragged on. Siobhan enjoyed spending a day watching television and flipping through the channels. I amused myself by uploading my photos from the camera onto the laptop and taking photos out of the hotel window.

A rest day such as this was probably a good thing. Driving continuously, day after day, was a bit tiring. I came up with a great idea for a Reality TV Show.

TV SHOW – The Great Cape to Cairo Safari

A team consists of a parent and a teenager 13-17. The parent is only allowed to drive between 7am and 7pm for safety reasons. The teenager is not allowed to drive. The object is to get from Cape Town to Cairo. The proposed route must be handed in before the race, so the TV Station organising the race can organise visas and make sure support vehicles will be following in each country.

Each team will be given $20 000 for fuel and accommodation along the way, a Sony Handy Cam, satellite phone/computer, a camera and a new 4x4. The first team to reach Cairo wins the million dollar prize. With money left over from the $20 000 given for fuel and accommodation, teams can buy time. For example, $500 buys you 12 hours which will be deducted from your total time. One of the large camera companies or National Geographic can also sponsor an Amazing Photo Competition as well, of photos taken along the way.

The teenager will be the navigator and cameraman. Each day's footage will be sent to the TV Station via satellite each night. The TV Station will then go through the footage and take out clips to make each episode.

The big benefit for the contestants, are that the parent and teenager will get to spend quality time together, which is something quite difficult to do in today's busy world. I know that I was quite surprised to discover that Siobhan was actually quite fun, did have a sense of humour and could be entertaining. Besides the quality time, contestants will also get a chance to see the real Africa, not just the tourist high spots. The viewers will get to see the interactions between parent and teenager which can be amusing, as well as the real Africa. I think it's a cool idea. Obviously, the TV Station will need to find quite a lot of sponsorship. For instance, a car company to provide the 4x4's; camera company for camera and handy cam; satellite phone company for phone and laptop; some company to sponsor the purchase of visas, fuel and accommodation money and also the support teams. Then money would have to be found to transport the cars back at the end.

The teams would be liable for paying all speeding fines, road infringements and entry fees. This can add up when driving in Africa if you are a demon on the road. This would come out of the $20 000. Prospective teams would have to send in audition tapes. It would be great if this could be a global competition, with teams travelling from all over the world to participate.

Anyway, just an idea. Sometimes I spend so much time thinking out of the box, I forget how to get back in.

Day Twelve: Mbeya to Mikumi

It took until midday for the money my friend sent me to show up on my phone. Vodacom, the phone company, let's people send money over the phone called Mpesa. You get the message on your phone someone has sent you money and you get a special password. You take your phone to the nearest Vodacom Shop, show them the password and text and you get the cash. Isn't modern technology amazing?

We checked out the hotel, filled up the tank and oil which was also empty and started on the 340km drive to Iringa. In the day when we looked to our right, we could see the size and scope of the mountains we'd struggled up two nights before.

By the time we were 20km from Mbeya, we'd driven through five road blocks and been caught by one speed camera. It was obviously a manic Monday for the traffic officials. Maybe they had a target to meet and they were behind and had been given the Monday to catch up. The traffic cop initially demanded 40 000 TSH, saying that the price of speeding fines had gone up. I had already left the village where we were supposed to slow down and was already on the open road, so technically, I wasn't speeding. But the cop pointed to the speed limit sign on the other side of the road indicating that drivers on that side of the road should slow down as they were approaching a village. Unfortunately, that sign faces the other way so you cannot read it on your side of the road. But that for him meant that I was still in a 50km/h area and I'd been doing 60km/h. I managed to talk him down to only fining me 20 000 TSH. Money was a bit tight at this stage of the game. 100km from Mbeya I got caught by another speed camera. Again, the cop wanted 40 000 TSH, but I managed to get away with only paying 10 000 TSH. Of course the money goes straight into their pockets; they don't give you any receipt or write out a fine! Corruption rules the roads in Tanzania! The 30 000 TSH left a severe dent in my remaining supply of cash, and I hoped to hell those speeding fines weren't going to come back and bite me in the bum.

We decided to bypass Iringa purely because there was no way Missy would make it up the steep hill to get to the town. Also, time was at a premium. We'd left Mbeya later than I'd wanted. The road after Iringa was excellent; all the roadworks having been completed in the one and a half months we'd been away. After driving through a total of fourteen roadblocks, we eventually reached Mikumi at 8pm.

It seemed as if every trucker on the road in Tanzania was staying in Mikumi for the night. We drove around for 30 minutes trying different guesthouses. Most were fleabags but all were full. Of course only the expensive ones we couldn't afford had rooms available! With the car low on petrol, I pulled into a fuel station. They had no fuel! Typical! When things are going badly for you it affects everything. We were just about to give up and chance driving through the Mikumi Game Park at night when we saw a sign advertising the Chella Lodge and Campsite. Really, all the lodge is, is one en suite room. The decor and interior of the bedroom was a pleasant surprise; very nice indeed. The bathroom was large, looked nice, but had no water or toilet paper, which does defeat the object of it being a bathroom. They wanted 35 000 TSH a night, but we said we didn't need breakfast so got it for 30 000 TSH which is around $20. The parking was very secure with a locked gate and guard. They even had DSTV.

RECIPES FROM AFRICA - Tanzania

Samaki Wa Nazi

Absolutely scrumptious, this tasty fish curry will have you crying out for more.

Ingredients

1kg firm fish
Salt and pepper to taste
3 tablespoons cooking oil
1 medium onion sliced into rings
2 cloves of garlic crushed or finely chopped
1 tablespoon curry powder
2 tablespoons tomato paste
2 red chillies finely chopped
Juice from ½ lemon
500ml coconut milk

Method

1. Season the fish with salt and pepper.
2. Heat the oil in a pan and brown the fish.
3. Remove the fish and keep it warm for the moment.
4. Use the same oil to fry the onion until brown.
5. Add the garlic, curry powder, chillies and lemon juice.
6. Mix well and stir while it cooks for two minutes.
7. Add the coconut milk and stir until it boils.
8. Put the warm fish into the mixture and simmer for about ten minutes.
9. Serve with rice.

Chella Lodge
Mikumi

The room was a pleasant surprise after driving around looking for a place to spend the night. The bathroom didn't have water or toilet paper. The bed didn't have a blanket but was very comfortable. Given the secure parking, $20 a night was still a bargain.

Stats for the day					
Odometer Start	**Odometer Finish**	**Day's Kilometres**	**Depart Time**	**Arrive Time**	**Hours travel**
188955	189492	537km	12h00	20h00	8 hours
Fuel	**Cost local currency**	**Cost US$**	**Accommodation**	**Cost local currency**	**Cost US$**
90.74 litres	161510 TSH	$107.32	Chella Lodge	30000 TSH	$19.93

Day Thirteen: Mikumi to Moshi

Surprisingly enough, we woke up the next morning. We'd been so cold during the night without blankets, we'd been convinced we'd freeze to death. We left early while it was still dark. Even without the car heater working, we'd still be warmer in the car than in that room. We tried a different fuel station and luckily they had fuel. Unfortunately, the gauge on the fuel pump wasn't working, so we could see how much fuel was going in, but the pump attendant used the calculator on his phone to calculate how much we should pay. It was only when I got Siobhan to work out the cost of the fuel on her phone later on in the day, that I realised we'd been diddled and charged for 20 more litres than had been put in. Given our current financial situation, this was a huge blow and would cost us dearly.

Driving through Mikumi park is a delight, especially at sunrise. You see so many animals it's unbelievable and really feel like you are somewhere out in the wild. Which I suppose you are.

The highlight of the drive through the park and in actual fact the whole day, was when we had to stop the car for a lion crossing the road. We tracked the lion with the camera as it walked majestically through the bush. Another car appeared on the horizon and stopped to look at the lion. The fool in the car opened his window and started filming the lion with his camera phone, shouting and jeering so that the lion stopped, looked ready to pounce, then turned tail and disappeared into the bush. Obviously, that guy in the car was a keen conservationist!

The **Mikumi National Park** is 3,230 sq km, the fourth-largest park in Tanzania, and part of a much larger ecosystem centred on the uniquely vast Selous Game Reserve. Hippos are the star attraction of the pair of pools situated 5km north of the main entrance gate. More than 400 bird species have been recorded in the park. While lions, giraffes, elephants, zebra, impala, kudu, sable antelope and buffalo are usually spotted, the park is most known for being the most reliable place in Tanzania for sightings of the powerful eland, the world's largest antelope.

Nothing beats seeing animals in the wild in their natural surroundings. After having visited numerous game parks and reserves over the years, I find that I can't stomach going to a zoo. Seeing an animal caged like that, its dignity taken away, just breaks my heart. The only thing worse that seeing a lion in a zoo, was having the misfortune to see African lions shivering at -36 degrees Celsius in a Siberian Tiger Park in Haerbin in Northern China.

By the time we reached Morogoro and used the last of our cash to put petrol in the car, we knew we were in trouble. Siobhan had agreed to forgo eating and buying lunch and had contributed her lunch money to the fuel budget. We needed a full tank to make it back all the way to Moshi, and

a three quarter tank would not make it. I'm not sure if it is the height above sea level or the quality of the petrol, but my car is a lot heavier on fuel in Tanzania. The two speeding fines and missing 20 litres at Mikumi were going to cost us big time. I decided all we could do was drive and see how far we got.

After driving for 100km with the fuel light on between Korogwe and Same, I knew that there was no way we'd make the last 120km to Moshi. We were so close, it was so unfair! Putting my pride in my back pocket, I stopped at a fuel station in Same and offered my camera as security in exchange for putting 50 litres of petrol into Missy's fuel tank. Surprisingly enough, the woman owner of the fuel station agreed. I made sure I removed the memory card from the camera first, handed her my proof copy of 'Fighting Fisi' as a gift for her child and promised to be back in a couple of days to pay her for the 50 litres and get my camera back.

The last 120km to Moshi were uneventful. All in all, we'd driven through 15 road blocks from Mikumi to Moshi, spotted three speed cameras and avoided getting any further fines, which in Tanzania is quite an accomplishment! As we approached Moshi we launched into song singing 'Jambo Bwana.' One of the first Kiswahili songs we'd learned. The feeling of arriving home safely was enough to bring tears to our eyes.

We had done it! A mother and daughter team, we'd driven all the way from Kilimanjaro to Table Mountain and back again. A total of 11 980km! The best part of it all was that we had got to spend a lot of time together, got to know each other better and hadn't killed each other. We became friends. My dream now, is to drive from Kilimanjaro to Cairo, but that might be more complicated and for that I'll probably need a new car. My ultimate dream, is to drive around the coast of Africa. That I'll only be able to do when I win the lottery!

Safari Njema! Good Travels!

Stats for the day					
Odometer Start	Odometer Finish	Day's Kilometres	Depart Time	Arrive Time	Hours travel
189492	190183	691km	06h30	16h30	10 hours
Fuel	Cost local currency	Cost US$	Accommodation	Cost local currency	Cost US$
116.22 litres	289000 TSH	$192.03	Home	0	0

Last Word

Life is like an African road, full of speed bumps, road blocks, potholes, wandering animals, unexpected bends, slow trucks and careering over-laden buses. But if you never take that road you'll miss out on the breathtaking scenery and friendly vibrant people you meet along the way.

My children have often said to me, "Why don't we just fly somewhere and stay in a holiday resort like normal people do?" I think if we ever did that, they might be bored. Travelling on a limited budget, using local transport, staying in cheap guesthouses, gives you a much richer experience than you'd get staying in a resort. I'd even go to say that travelling on the cheap gives you the wildest adventures.

We could have completed the trip in a couple of days if we just drove solidly day and night and didn't stop to look at the scenery. But the way we did it, only travelling about 500km a day, turned the down and up trip into a holiday. It gave me an opportunity to take time out of my busy life to get to know my teenage daughter, and discover that she is an entertaining, friendly, lovely young girl, and not just the sulky, angry teenager I see at home when I ask her to pick her mess up off the floor.

It's hard to believe that we travelled a total of 11 980km! Here are some of our stats for the trip.

Stats for down trip			
Odometer Start	**Odometer Finish**	**Total Kilometres**	**Total Days Traveled**
176301	181926	5625km	9 days
Total Fuel Consumed		**Total Fuel Cost US$**	**Total Accommodation Cost US$**
787.55 litres		$938.04	$494.29
Stats for up trip			
Odometer Start	**Odometer Finish**	**Total Kilometres**	**Total Days Traveled**
183828	190183	6355km	12 + 1 rest day
Total Fuel Consumed		**Total Fuel Cost US$**	**Total Accommodation Cost US$**
816.18 litres		$1099.24	$439.70

Total Stats			
Odometer Start	**Odometer Finish**	**Total Kilometres**	**Total Days Traveled**
176301	190183	13882km (includes 1902km traveled around Cape Town) 11980km on down and up drive	21 days + 1 rest day
Total Fuel Consumed		**Total Fuel Cost US$**	**Total Accommodation Cost US$**
1603.73 litres		$2037.28	$933.99

Our biggest cost was obviously that of fuel, and if we had a more fuel-efficient vehicle it would have been much less. It would have been much cheaper to fly directly from Kilimanjaro Airport to Cape Town International Airport, but then we would have just flown over the six different countries we visited, and not seen anything of their magnificent scenery or met their friendly people. The trip was worth it. Definitely a once-in-a-lifetime experience, and I'm all for those!

When Siobhan and I sat down when it was all over and reflected on the trip, we decided that we should give some Accommodation Awards. We stayed in so many different standards of accommodation, that it is only fair that we give credit where it is due and acknowledge those establishments that were outstanding in some way. Some of our choices were hard to make as there was some stiff competition. Others stood out.

ACCOMMODATION AWARDS

Most Luxurious: Protea Safari Lodge, Lusaka
Most Unfriendly: Rhino Motel, Morogoro
Best Dinner: Chantler's Lodge, Livingstone
Best value for money: Rift Valley Hotel, Mbeya
Best Vibe: The Big Blue Backpackers, Nkhata Bay
Most Helpful: Kasasa Club, Dwangwa
Best Breakfast: Protea Safari Lodge, Lusaka
Most Fleabag: Rhino Motel, Morogoro
Most Professional: Protea Safari Lodge, Lusaka
Best Bathroom: Protea Safari Lodge, Lusaka
Worst Bathroom: Zebra Inn Backpackers, Louis Trichardt
Most Over-priced: Chevron Hotel, Masvingo

Best Bed: Comfort Lodge, Lusaka
Best Decor: Marang Hotel, Francistown
Best Holiday Deal: The Big Blue Backpackers, Nkhata Bay
Best Smile: Chef at Chipata Motel, Chipata
Most Welcoming: Marang Hotel, Francistown
Best Room Service: Protea Safari Lodge, Lusaka

Was the trip worth it? Most definitely! I would do it again in a heartbeat. A road trip such as this is the best way to see another country and experience its culture. Hopefully, I still have many more road trips such as this one, coming up in my future!

Acclaim for Cindy Vine

Stop the world, I need to pee! 'A fun read with an underlying question for us all.' Janet Aston

Fear, Phobias and Frozen Feet (written as Cindy van den Heuvel) 'What I think is great about this book as well is the fact that the author does bring it to a down to earth level by cutting to the core or root of the problem itself. And there is no discrimination here, she lets you know that both Men and Women face these scenarios day to day. I would advise all my friends to read this book because in reality we see these cases more too often in this world we are living in. I definitely give this 5 Stars!' JJRUBIO

The Case of Billy B 'A worthwhile read that will have you turning pages and biting your nails.' Suzanne Wheeler

'A classic story of the human struggle. The author's descriptive prose delves deeply and is very emotional.
It is a recommended read.' PB

'The Case of Billy B is a unique, well-written, and emotionally resonant read. I got so wrapped up in the story that I finished the last 160 pages in a single afternoon!' T.R. Braxton

'In The Case of Billy B, author Cindy Vine weaves a heartwarming, enduring, and poignant story that will leave a soft place in your heart.' Keleigh Hadley

'I had tears in my eyes.' Reader's Favorite

Not Telling 'Couldn't put this book down. Read it in one evening. The book takes you on a rollercoaster ride through the life of the main character. Very emotionally disturbing experiences. You really feel connected to her and her life; and hope that things will start going her way.' Rebecca on Goodreads

'Not Telling was a great book. I couldn't put it down, I got sucked in within the first 2 pages. You should definitely read it if you haven't already.' Ashley Fortner on Goodreads